Sprint Recruiting

Copyright © 2021 Trent Cotton

All rights reserved.

Table of Contents

Acknowledgments 3

The Problem with Traditional Recruiting 5

What's Agile and SCRUM got to do with it? 18

The Business Defines the Priority 30

    How to implement the Point System 37

Work In Progress (WIP) Limits Drive Focus 46

    WIP Guidelines 55

    The Importance of Time Blocking 56

The Sprint Provides Efficiency 65

    Definition of Sprint 68

    Steps to implement your sprint 73

        Define the length of your Sprint 73

        Define The Sprint Workflow 74

        Have a Sprint Zero 76

        Set up your reporting 77

        Key Points to Remember for Sprints 79

Feedback drives Progress 80

    Setting a deadline for feedback. 82

    Candidate Feedback 91

    Mindset to avoid 93

    Radical Candor Feedback 94

The Mindset Shift 98

The Sprint Recruiting Mechanics 116

    Measure what counts 116

    Create your meeting schedules 122

Final Thoughts-Answering WHY? 133

In their own words 137
Bibliography 144

Acknowledgments

Early in my career, I learned the value of working with a team that accepted me for who I am. I often struggled with belonging because I am different. I thought differently, challenged the status quo, and found ways to stand out, even when it brought more scrutiny.
It led me on a journey to find a group of people who would embrace and endure my outlandish ideas and obsession with iterative efficiency.

It's been a long search, but I can finally say I've found my home with the fantastic team you will meet throughout this book. They have been supportive of the idea of Sprint Recruiting from its inception, throughout its struggles, and continue to help refine our methodology. They've been my harshest critics and most prolific cheerleaders over the last two years. The Sprint Recruiting Methodology is not something I could have done alone. This team is interwoven into the fabric of its success. I would be remiss if I did not acknowledge the blood, sweat, and tears they've poured into its success.

I'd also like to acknowledge and thank my leadership team, who have given me free rein to break ideologies, processes, and system thinking to find something better. They've given me the training to think differently, the latitude to consistently search for excellence, and the cover fire I've needed from time to time. The ability to work for an organization that embraces a "fail fast and learns quickly" culture has allowed my team and me to thrive in a very tumultuous transition over the last two years.

When I stop and take a moment to reflect, I have it all. I'm surrounded by incredible professionals who not only accept me for who I am but challenge me to continue to evolve. I work for an organization that supports crazy ideas and permits us to fail. It's one of the reasons I have made our firm home over the last ten years and why I rarely search for another opportunity.

When you've found a home, you tend not to want to leave. That is how I feel about my team. It's how I feel about the management team that supports me. It's how I feel about an organization that's transformed me and allowed me to be a part of its transformation. This is a theme you will read throughout the rest of this book, and it's why I'd like to take the first page of the story to dedicate it to all of them. Without them, there would be no story to tell.

They are, after all, the best part of it all!

The Problem with Traditional Recruiting

I was excited when I entered the recruiting industry in 2004. My previous years as a banker taught me how building relationships, pipelines, and strategies could make anyone successful in any industry. I was eager to put my theory to the test. In 2017, I began doubting whether I desired to continue or whether I had what it took to be a successful recruiter. I was accustomed to demanding and often unrealistic clients, but the previous six months had beaten me into a depression.

The industry changed a lot over 16 years. When I began, LinkedIn wasn't a thing, so I had to call into banks to build lists of talent to target. I couldn't just ping someone on LinkedIn and have their resume at my fingertips. It was hard work in the beginning, but I freaking loved it. The challenge taught me how to hone my skills and develop relationships with not only my internal clients but also my candidates.

My goal in recruiting was always to please the client. I thought focusing on lessening the time to fill would do it, but it didn't. I thought focusing on more communication would do the trick-no that didn't do it either. I tried every "one-stop" trick I knew but always came up short in delivering more candidates to the right jobs in the shortest amount of time.

Focusing on the goals only seemed to increase my burnout and diverted my focus into too many rabbit holes. When I shifted my thought process to focus on the process, I immediately began identifying gaps, roadblocks, black holes, and a whole array of other impediments standing in the way of how I defined success.

I had lost my resolve and my mind. I felt like Sisyphus who was punished by the gods, forced to push a massive rock up a mountain only to have it roll back down the following morning. I've read enough leadership and breakthrough books to know when you are at your breaking point; the tide is about to turn. I just had to push through and find my groove again.

The standard way of recruiting (which I will refer to as traditional recruiting) is sometimes the very definition of insanity. You get a job, you search for candidates, conduct interviews, place the candidate, they quit, and the cycle repeats.

Let's discuss some of the issues and landmines along the journey for recruiters.

Unmanaged Expectations

Hiring managers can be unrealistic, but in most cases, this is the recruiter's fault. To please and dazzle our hiring managers, we rarely manage their expectations. Let's not forget the job description of the purple squirrel that every manager dreams up. They want someone with perfect skills and experience with a budget that would barely afford a recent college graduate. Most of us kick into the "I'm going to rock your world" mindset and become hell-bent on finding that elusive candidate. Meanwhile, hiring managers wait like a disgruntled old person in the line at the DMV.

If you are not defining the process with your hiring managers, you will fall prey to their expectations.

Talent Shortage

Jobvite Recruiter Nation Report suggests that only 67% of the recruiters search for candidates with relevant job experience. There is a shift in many companies, including my current employer, to search more based on competencies and acumen versus relevant job experience. Finding the right employee that fits the criteria makes the hiring procedure a daunting task if you are still recruiting using the traditional methodology.

The genuinely sexy, in-demand jobs are the toughest because there are usually ten firms looking for the same talent profile. Recruiters are feverishly working to find the talent, engage them in the selection process, and some cases, convince the hiring manager the talent is the right person for the job. There are some serious challenges, including talent shortages, skills gaps, and location issues. If that doesn't stress you out, then globalization should; companies are fighting for talent in a candidate-driven market for candidates who are smarter and have more information available to them than ever before.

The Process

I've worked for several medium and large corporations, and one thing is true in all of them: ***There's no such thing as an easy hiring process.***

Regulations, antiquated hiring protocols, and untrained managers are just some of the obstacles rarely addressed. After all, we have to be polite and not let anyone in the process get their feelings hurt, right?

Where there is process overload in many organizations, there are also gross inefficiencies. The fast-paced world of recruiting leaves little time to stop and address what is and is not working. Teams continue the madness week to week, hoping to make process improvements in the future. But that day never comes. The continuous, iterative compilation of inefficiencies creates a drag on the candidate experience and recruiter engagement if it is not addressed.

Strategy

Every recruiter claims to be a strategic recruiter, but the traditional model makes it nearly impossible. Competing priorities and the lack of focus inhibit recruiters from accomplishing their goal to be strategic. Eliminate the distraction of "every job is a priority" to allow the recruiter to spend more time focused on what will move the needle versus which job has the hiring manager with the loudest voice.

As the team focused on our client's top roles, we spent more time sourcing and less time being reactive. We began to find great candidates who were not fit for the critical role in the sprint but an excellent fit for the organization. The goldmine in recruiting is to have that perfect candidate in your pocket for the ideal position. Unfortunately, traditional recruiting does not allow the time to develop these talent pipelines.

Collaboration with your Client

One of the most frustrating aspects of traditional recruiting is the long (if existent) feedback loop with our clients. We would think we'd be on the right track only to find out four weeks into the search that the manager had changed the requirements for the job.

It is common to come across the "wait and see" procedure. A recent study indicated 56% of the recruiters stated that they could not make the right hires due to the lengthy hiring procedure.

As I thought over the issues I was encountering, I realized there were some common themes to my frustrations. The constant problems with the traditional recruiting process include:

- Everything is a priority (which means nothing is a priority)
- The gap between client expectation and reality
- Focus on the wrong metrics in the recruiting process
- Chaotic communication, disillusionment, and burnout
- Lack of focus on what matters
- Lack of a defined strategy and process

Traditional recruiting is sometimes the very definition of insanity. You get a job, you search for candidates, conduct interviews, place the candidate, they quit, and the cycle repeats. I narrowed the real problems to four main pitfalls of traditional recruiting I wanted to address:

- Lack of prioritization
- Lack of focus
- Misalignment of client needs versus our ability to meet them
- A chaotic, one-way feedback loop

Lack of Prioritization

At the time, I supported a business executive who had a new priority job every week, sometimes twice a week. It was a "hair on fire" or "have to have this filled" scenario every week. This constant change in direction for the team created a ton of stress and drained our efficiency ratio. Rather than completing one job, we were consistently diverted to the latest dumpster fire at his direction. We lost credibility with our candidates, who got lost in the process while our morale began to tank, and we took the stress out on each other.

As our priorities kept changing, we missed out on many opportunities to add great talent to the firm. The forced multitasking created holes in our candidate experience. We were so unorganized that we often didn't realize just how many candidates we lost in our chaos until it was too late. The definition of success was changing so often, it seemed pointless to attempt to please our client. Our client was essentially driving a bus to the looney bin once a week, and we willingly got on the bus with him. It was insanity, and just writing about it causes my anxiety levels to increase.

Lack of Focus

When I dove into the data during the initial development phase of Sprint Recruiting, I noticed that we would often work on roles for weeks on end when we had already presented a slew of qualified candidates to the managers for review. This continuous chaos kept us from working on other positions that needed attention and created a bottleneck.

Managers would have over-analysis paralysis or the fear of missing out (FOMO) of another great candidate who may or may not exist. We were creating more work for ourselves and killing our efficiency in the process. It was as if we were trying to build a car but kept focusing on creating more doors when focusing on building out the engine or some other essential element would be more beneficial. We had no process identifying when to stop funneling candidates to the managers and moving on to different roles.

We called ourselves multitasking when we were creating more work for ourselves while also sabotaging our candidate experience. Nothing will kill team engagement like a client who continuously wants to badger you for more candidates when they potentially have a rockstar already in the pool. Without any rule or process to create a stop-gap, we continuously fell into the trap of just being busy.

The One-Way Feedback Loop

I noticed we had a one-sided feedback service level agreement (SLA). Clients could demand time limits on our team, but we didn't do the same to them, adding to the over-analysis paralysis or FOMO mentioned above.

Candidates would go through the process with little or no feedback unless they were the chosen ones to receive an offer. As a result, we missed out on qualified candidates who may have been great for other roles in the organization. Was the candidate too inexperienced or not a culture fit? Most of the time, we only received minimal feedback, which would tell us the candidate just wasn't the one for the role.

When I charted the candidate journey using data from our applicant tracking system, one of our departments took an average of 7 business days to tell us if a submitted candidate was worthy of an interview and another two weeks to get feedback after an interview. This added three weeks to the candidate process in a candidate-driven market. Without some time of requirement or time limit, we continued to suffer a bad reputation in the market for a belabored interview process and ghosting candidates who were not selected for the role.

Not Aligned with our Client's Needs

I frequently heard client feedback that recruiting could not meet their needs. When I would pull the numbers, I could see that in a selected month, we filled X number of positions, which seemed impressive as a solo data point. The client's feedback tended to include that the roles filled were not aligned with the business's needs. Without prioritization and a belabored feedback loop, it made sense why this was such a contention point with our clients.

I also noticed we had no way to stop and evaluate the process consistently. We would jump on the rat wheel of insanity day after day without stopping to identify what was working and what obstacles prevented success. Sometimes, we would have the one-off meeting as a team, but without client involvement. How would we know if the ideas we created were feasible?

When we tried to set up regular meetings with our clients, some would just blow them off or indicate they had more important meetings to attend. It was not as though we were not trying; it was more like we didn't have their buy-in to the iterative process of success. Honestly, if their view of our process was that it prohibited them from meeting their goals and produced lackluster candidates, why would they want to waste their time meeting with us to enhance the process?

What I wanted was a Recruiting Utopia, but what I found myself working in Recruiting Shit Show. I knew there had to be a solution out there but found myself too exhausted and disengaged to give it any more effort.

In 2017, I received training on the Agile Methodology. I became intrigued with how companies like Apple, Google, and Facebook leveraged it to create products faster and more efficiently. I decided to listen to the book SCRUM, written by Jeff Sutherland, to make our recruiting efforts more Agile. As he read his manifesto on SCRUM, the wheels started turning. I realized many of the constraints addressed by Agile in software development could easily be applied to recruiting. Honestly, I don't remember the last two hours of my drive because of the fireworks of creativity firing off in my head. I was so excited and revitalized by the ideas that I could hardly wait to get to my office and start hashing out Sprint Recruiting.

I wanted to create a relatively simple and address some critical issues in the process. My goal was to find a way to meet the needs I felt were as crucial as the recruiting leader for my organization:

- Equal accountability between the recruiter and the client
- Focus on what will bring value to the client
- Constant contact with each role
- Prioritization
- Gamification of the system to help move projects to completion
- Measurable results with a focus on what matters

Let's go back to my goal: create a recruiting utopia! In my search for the solution, I found an interesting example of team efficiency in nature. I'll confess, I'm a nerd, so I'm always reading random material to identify better ways to increase efficiency on the team. I stumbled upon an article explaining why geese flew in a V formation and the science behind why their behavioral instinct made them such a great example of efficiency.

First, it conserves their energy. Each bird flies slightly above the bird in front of him, resulting in a reduction of wind resistance. The birds take turns being in the front, falling back when they get tired. In this way, the geese can fly long distances before they stop for rest. The authors of a 2001 *Nature* article stated that pelicans that fly alone beat their wings more frequently and have higher heart rates than those that fly in formation. It follows that birds that fly in formation glide more often and reduce energy expenditure (Weimerskirch, 2001).

The second benefit to the V formation is that it is easy to keep track of every bird in the group. Flying in a formation may assist with the communication and coordination within the group. Fighter pilots often use this formation for the same reason. If you have ever watched a group of geese flies overhead, you've probably heard them grunting and squawking at each other as they pass. This loud interchange is feedback exchange to ensure each goose is fulfilling their role in the team.

One of the most interesting aspects of geese behavior is the intuitive nature of their efficiency. Their ability to fly long distances compared to their counterparts is primarily due to their teamwork efficiency. It's a complicated process made to look effortless.

I decided to follow the goose's lead and began thinking about redesigning our recruiting methodology to function more like geese and less like a chaotic flock of birds. I had my four pitfalls of traditional recruiting already identified, so I decided to start there. For each pitfall, I researched how Agile organizations and teams addressed a similar issue. It took a couple of weeks, but I developed the four principles of Sprint Recruiting.

1. The business defines the priority using a point system.
2. We will use Work in Progress Limits to keep our focus and create a recruiting rhythm.
3. Our two-week sprint will allow us to increase our focus and take time to innovate, iterate, and accelerate our recruiting efforts.
4. A 48-hour deadline for feedback would enable us to move quicker on candidates and quickly redefine our search strategies if needed.

Imagine being able to start your planning for two weeks focused on your business unit's 5-6 top roles versus the twenty or thirty it may have open. The overwhelming distraction commonly associated with high requisition loads subsides as you focus on the most critical, manageable requisition list for two weeks. As you make progress on your top priority role by meeting a minimum number of qualified candidates scheduled with the manager, you move on to the next one in priority. You'll continuously follow this format until you find a methodological approach to getting things done efficiently.

Much like the geese flying in a V formation, feedback is constant and keeps the process moving. The feedback from your managers moves candidates quickly through the process. Communication among your team members helps work be prioritized and allocated to resources with the capacity to meet the goal of the two-week sprint. Feedback allows the group to adjust to changes in the industry or client demand quicker and more efficiently. The stress most feel in the traditional recruiting model has been mitigated by what I call the "sprint instinct." Like geese, you and your team begin to use resistance as a way to push forward with less energy.

Most importantly, your clients begin to understand the process, and finally, you have a common language to use to communicate progress and obstacles. The typical pain points of time to fill and the number of open jobs is replaced with an obsession by you and your clients to make progress on the most critical roles. This obsession also allows you to take the time to truly focus on these roles to find more qualified candidates with more time to source. Traditional recruiting forces recruiters to move each job a little every day; sprint recruiting allows you and your team to make massive moves on fewer critical roles over two weeks.

What if you could start your day reviewing a dashboard of ranked jobs with separate swim lanes that show how many candidates are in the process. Get ready for the relief you will feel when you realize the most critical jobs in the sprint all are at a point where you are waiting on feedback on interviews, so you begin getting a jump-start from the other positions. The feeling of working more efficiently and effortlessly will become addictive. The ability to end the day and measure the progress you've made will be rewarding and allow you to be present with loved ones when deciding to finish work for the day.

Sprint Recruiting was born from the chaos of traditional recruiting. Our process has become more efficient with each iteration, and our engagement with both managers and candidates increased proportionally. The four principles of Sprint Recruiting evolved through this process as we continued to innovate, iterate, and accelerate from Sprint to Sprint.

The Business Defines the Priority

If you are not defining the prioritization of work with your hiring managers, you will fall prey to their expectations. Sprint Recruiting forces the client to prioritize the work using a budget of points. Rather than "every position is important," the client will be forced to rank positions to identify the top 3-5 positions requiring the most focus during a sprint. If this rule is violated or ignored, the rest of the process will not work, and you will only be applying a new name to your old, outdated recruiting process.

The Sprint Provides Efficiency

Sprint is the critical adjective in Sprint Recruiting. The sprint allows you to measure activity in a shorter, defined period of time to determine what worked and what didn't. The goal is to scale what worked into the following sprints while also discussing potential solutions for the obstacles experienced. This process helps curtail the typical insanity of doing the same repeatedly, over without optimizing lessons learned.

The typical sprint term we will use in this book is two weeks. Every organization is different, so if you need your sprint to be shorter or longer, it is entirely up to you.

Work In Progress (WIP) Limits Drive Focus

WIP limits allow recruiters to follow the pull method versus the push method commonly used by the old recruiting model. WIP limits should be set by and agreed upon by both your client and the recruiting team. This helps recruiters develop a rhythm to recruiting during the sprint and forms a "stop" measure to help them know when to move on to the next job in the priority listing.

We will discuss swimlanes later in the book.

Feedback Drives Progress

Once the WIP limits are in place, you can let the feedback be the catalyst for progress. Old recruiting methods will typically place all of the recruiting responsibility on the recruiter. Sprint Recruiting puts just as much accountability on the hiring manager does the recruiter, creating a partnership.

A lack of hiring manager feedback combined with hitting a WIP limit for the job becomes a quantifiable roadblock. Similarly, when a recruiter sends more candidates to the manager to review than the WIP limit allows, the fault is on the recruiter ruining the process, not the manager. Sprint Recruiting not only places the work where it needs to go in the order it needs to go but also puts the blame where it belongs to foster the excellent communication required to keep the needle moving in a positive direction.

Four rules to live by. Nothing drastic but these are non-negotiable truths as you begin your journey into Sprint Recruiting.

I know this sounds like a dream now but let me assure you that it can be a reality for you if you follow this book's steps. Sure, my team still has times we find ourselves in a frenzy due to business demand, but it's manageable now. When we get stressed, we go back to the sprint principles and realign our focus on efficiency. Sprint recruiting has made us closer as a team and increased the value we bring to our organization.

The Sprint Recruiting methodology is my attempt to address each of these with an easy to follow, cohesive process to execute for both the recruiters and clients. The book will not be a long, exhaustive dissertation on the methodology. My goal is to give you the necessary information for you and your team to implement this successful recruiting methodology without all of the extra fluff typically found in other books. The core of sprint recruiting is efficiency, so why shouldn't the book be the same, right?

There's a helpful graphic of these rules you can download on the SprintRecruiting.com website under the Resources page. Be sure to share this with your team and your client to help the Sprint Recruiting implementation process be successful. I'm excited to teach you each of the principles and share our journey with you.

Get ready. Your recruiting utopia is within your reach. Let's dive in.

What's Agile and SCRUM got to do with it?

It's a very linear process. Each of these steps represents a distinct stage of the process, and each stage generally finishes before the next one can begin. There is typically a stage-gate between each. The most frustrating pitfall of the method is that the project's requirements are rarely met at the beginning of the project. Additionally, the client is usually not at the center of the process, so you run the risk of delivering a product the end-user will not use.

If you need an example, think of any government project. Time is spent building the requirements, and months are spent documenting all of these requirements to form beautiful mounds of manuals that no one reads. A timeline of underestimated deliverables and cost estimates are grossly unrealistic.

The Agile methodology is different. Work is evaluated when **completed**, not at the end of the project. Teams consist of interdisciplinary members. It moves in time blocks or sprints, enabling a more precise focus on objectives to be completed.

Here are eight benefits of Agile Provided by Segue Tech:
- **Stakeholder Engagement**
  - Agile provides multiple opportunities for stakeholder and team engagement – before, during, and after each Sprint. Involving the client in every step increases the collaboration between the client and the project team. The primary benefit of this integration is the team's opportunities to understand the client's needs. It also develops trust in the team's ability to deliver high-quality working products. A natural byproduct of this process is a more engaged client.
- **Transparency**

- With the client, An Agile approach provides a unique opportunity for client involvement throughout the project, from prioritizing features to iteration planning and review sessions to frequent software builds containing new features. However, this also requires clients to understand that they see a work in progress in exchange for this added benefit of transparency.
- **Early and Predictable Delivery**
    - By using time-boxed, fixed schedule Sprints of 1-4 weeks, new features are delivered quickly and frequently, with a high predictability level. It allows companies to release or beta test the software earlier than planned if there is sufficient business value.
- **Predictable Costs and Schedule**
    - Because each Sprint is a fixed duration, the cost is predictable and limited to the team's work in the fixed-schedule time box. Combined with the client's estimates before each Sprint, the client can more readily understand each feature's approximate cost, which improves decision-making about the priority of features and the need for additional iterations.
- **Allows for Change**
    - While the team needs to stay focused on delivering an agreed-to subset of the product's features during each iteration, there is an opportunity to refine and reprioritize the overall product backlog continually. New or changed backlog items can be planned for the next iteration, providing the opportunity to introduce changes within a few weeks.
- **Focuses on Business Value**
    - By allowing the client to determine the priority of features, the team understands what's most important to the client's business. It can deliver the features that provide the most business value.

- **Focuses on Users**
    - Agile commonly uses user stories with business-focused acceptance criteria to define product features. By focusing on real users' needs, each element incrementally delivers value, not just an IT component. It also provides the opportunity to beta test software after each Sprint, gaining valuable feedback early in the project and providing the ability to make changes as needed.
- **Improves Quality**
    - By breaking down the project into manageable units, the project team can focus on high-quality development, testing, and collaboration. Also, by producing frequent builds and conducting testing and reviews during each iteration, quality is improved by finding and fixing defects quickly and identifying expectation mismatches early.
    - Agile allows for more fluidity, client buy-in, and agility in any process. Although mostly used in software development, I wondered how I could use the methodology to evolve recruiting.

The benefits listed above became my inspiration to take a hard look at how we were doing recruiting. As I thought through the value Agile brought organizations, I understood some pitfalls in traditional recruiting that could be overcome by a new recruiting model. What I lacked was how to create a process to implement the Agile methodology. I began researching SCRUM as a possible solution.

According to SCRUM.org, Scrum is a framework within which people can address complex adaptive problems while productively and creatively delivering products of the highest possible value. It is a simple framework for effective team collaboration on complex products and processes. If you'd like to watch a video showing how Scrum works in development, be sure to visit www.scrum.org and watch their YouTube video halfway through the homepage.

Think of Scrum as a process for Agile. An Agile Scrum process benefits the organization by helping it to
- Increase the quality of the deliverables
- Cope better with change as well as expect the changes
- Provide better estimates while spending less time creating them
- Have more control of the project schedule and state

The Scrum Team is a cross-functional team designed to move a project faster and more efficiently through the production process. Each product point or need is called a story. Think of a story as something to represent significant work that must be done to create a key design feature in a product. These requirements often, but not always, represent work to support the features a user would need for the product to be successful.

As an example, let's say we were building a mobile app for a small business client. They want a product to allow clients to know when sales are available, an online shopping feature to drive sales and a way for clients to communicate with the customer support team. In the traditional project management practice, each of these elements is documented using reams of paper and hundreds of required documentation. With a story, the massive project would be broken down into three main stories:
1. We're having a sale
2. Online store
3. Chat with customer support

The cross-functional teams will work together to identify the features and requirements for each story. Within each story, points are assigned a priority to each component providing a ranking of work during the Sprint. Rather than siloed teams working on one key element, Scrum allows the cross-functional team to use the points to determine when each team member will need to allocate their time to accomplish the feature they are responsible. The points also allow teams to determine the amount of work necessary for each element to help with resource allocation. It provides prioritization and a rhythm to the production process, making it more efficient and quicker to market.

Does this process work? Let's look at an example of how Salesforce.com used Agile and Scrum to transform their business.

Salesforce.com was founded in a San Francisco apartment in 1999. In the early days, setting and meeting deadlines were manageable since its R&D organization was so small. As the firm grew, and the complexity of cloud-based products increased, dates for significant releases began to see a drop in efficiency, creating obstacles to growth and low client reviews. By 2006, salesforce.com had gone from four releases per year down to just one because of its use of the outdated and ineffective waterfall project management.

In late 2006, the company implemented Agile and Scrum methodology to combat inefficiencies experienced due to its growth and inadequate project management processes. Within only a few months, Salesforce.com returned to a more regular delivery rhythm with fewer defects and, more importantly, on-time delivery. The time to market major releases had increased by 61 percent, and Salesforce.com's Net Promoter Score, a good indicator of customer satisfaction, rose to 94 percent.

Early on, the Agile rollout team also recognized the need to track and prioritize features to determine which fit into the proper iteration or Sprint. The team leveraged Scrum, which was essential to their desire to scale and coordinate multiple development teams across the R&D organization. The team developed a tracking tool to allow teams to identify each release's critical elements, the points assigned, and progress throughout the Sprint. They experienced more collaboration and communication between departments, which only added to the firm's ability to produce quality products.

While we all know how successful Salesforce.com is now, I think it's important to discuss the impact Agile and Scrum have on revenues. Many methodologies preach efficiency and client satisfaction, but it's always impressive to see the direct impact on a firm's ability to turn these ideas into profit. Salesforce.com's revenues for the fiscal year ending in

January 2006 topped $309 million. Once implementing Agile and increasing the ability to release enhancements more often and with fewer defects, its revenues jumped to $497 million just one year later. Two years later, Salesforce.com crossed the billion-dollar mark, recognizing 20% in revenues to $1.3 Billion.

This is just one of the many accounts of how companies have leveraged Agile and Scrum to enhance team engagement and efficiency and increase profits in incredible ways. It's why Scrum remains one of the most searched terms when someone Googles software or product development. There are numerous certification courses offered and even more online groups where professionals gather together to ask questions and swap best practices. This methodology is not a fad but the new reality of how companies can remain competitive and responsive to their clients' quickly changing needs.

Before we get into the mechanics of how Sprint Recruiting can transform your business, let's first outline the key roles and terms needed for your new recruiting methodology. Similar to Scrum, each position has a defined responsibility and is key to a successful implementation. I'll provide you the roles and responsibilities and help you think through who in your organization might be the best fit for each position based on our experiences.

Recruiting Leader
The recruiting leader in Sprint recruiting serves the same role as the SCRUM Master in Agile. The Scrum Master is the team role responsible for ensuring the team lives Agile values and principles and follows the processes and practices that the group agreed they would use.
The responsibilities of this role include:
- Clearing obstacles
- Establishing an environment where the team can be effective
- Addressing team dynamics
- Ensuring a good relationship between the team and sprint owner as well as others outside the team

- Protecting the team from outside interruptions and distractions.

As the recruiting leader, you have to keep the team moving toward filling those assigned points during the Sprint. You will find your schedule more consumed with identifying and overcoming obstacles versus chasing fires as you would in traditional recruiting. You will also be responsible for facilitating the daily standups and retro meetings with your team throughout the sprint process. In some cases, you may also be heavily involved in the client allocation calls as the leader if your team is not strong enough to lead them independently.

The recruiting leader is also the master of metrics for the Sprint. I spend the first part of most every day reviewing our dashboards ahead of our standup meetings to ensure I am aware of the progress made. Sometimes I'll ping my team before the call with a snapshot of the metrics and prepare them for critical roles I want to update during our standup. The sprint recruiting leader must be data-driven and data-informed to be most effective in this new recruiting framework.

One of the most critical roles the recruiting leader has is to hold everyone to the Sprint recruiting framework. I find myself redirecting both team members and partners out of the traditional recruiting mindset and back on the principles that make Sprint recruiting work. Some common questions I find helpful are:

- Why are we focused on a role that was not awarded points this Sprint? Have the priorities changed?
- How are you working during the week using the time blocking method?
- How many points away are we from 100%?
- Are we losing focus on the primary roles identified in this Sprint? If so, why and how do we fix it?

Believe it or not, I usually ask one or all of these questions throughout the Sprint, and we've been doing this for almost two years. I feel like a broken record, but I've found these questions help everyone redirect their focus back to how the client defines success in the sprint-the allocation of points. We'll spend more time discussing the mindset journey for leaders later in the book.

Product or Sprint Owner
The Sprint Owner (SO) is the key stakeholder for the project. Part of the Sprint Owner's responsibilities is to have a vision of what they wish to build and convey that vision to the scrum team. This is key to successfully starting any Agile software development project. The Agile Sprint Owner does this through the product backlog, a prioritized features list for the product.
Sprint Recruiting would make sense that the executive for a department or line of business would be the Sprint Owner (SO), but we discovered that was not always feasible. Some department leaders knew very little about the open roles' impacts on their division. Others were still traveling, which made it hard for us to have a bi-weekly allocation call with them.

Sprint Recruiting allows department leaders to designate the SO role to someone on the team who can prioritize work. The owner role requires an individual with specific skills and traits, including availability, proximity to the business needs, and communication skills. The best SOs show commitment by doing whatever is necessary to prioritize the work – and that means being actively engaged with their recruiting partners.

The SO has defined responsibilities in our methodology and must be committed to the success of the Sprint. Be sure to stay away from a SO who tends to consistently blame everyone else for their mistakes, as this will lead to trouble implementing Sprint Recruiting.

Here's a list of their key responsibilities to help you identify the best PO for the job.
- **Define the vision** - The Sprint Owner is the voice of the client and should be able to leverage their high-

level perspective to define goals and create a vision for your recruiting team. They are responsible for communicating with stakeholders, including your team, their fellow executives, and hiring managers, to ensure the goals are clear and the vision aligns with business objectives.

Having a Sprint Owner with a higher perspective ensures that the team maintains a cohesive vision despite Agile product development's flexible and often fast-paced nature. Everyone needs to be on the same page to work effectively, creating mutual accountability in the recruiting process.

- **Define the Priority** - The key role of the Sprint Owner is to prioritize needs. They must juggle the triangle of scope, budget, and time, weighing priorities according to stakeholders' needs and objectives. The recruiting team should communicate capacity needs or concerns openly with the SO to create a clear set of expectations during the Sprint.

  The SO takes budgeted points and assigns them to the critical roles in the Sprint. They are also the individuals who can designate a role as expedited since they will have more intimate knowledge of their organization's needs.

- **Providing Feedback** - You will need to be sure your SO is someone comfortable giving feedback, and the more candid, the better. They are your partner in this process, so they need to help you identify ways to become more efficient with every Sprint.

- **Equitable and Firm** -Your Sprint Owner will also need to have a backbone with their peers. They're not only responsible for holding the recruiting team accountable but also the business unit. They'll be the partner in the Sprint but should not show favoritism through the process. They are the voice of the client but not the ones responsible for giving excuses. If they are to hold you and your team to a definition of success, they keep their department to that same level. It's only when they are as firm with their colleagues as you are with your team that you'll begin to see the real power of this partnership.

Let me take a quick moment to sidebar just how important this partnership is with a little story.

We worked on this Big Whale (what our team called a 50 point or higher job) and began finding qualified candidates within three days of the sprint beginning. Unfortunately, our hiring manager went AWOL on us. I called, emailed, and instant messaged them to no avail. On day 7, I called the Sprint Owner for the line of business to realign priorities. The conversation went something like this:

Sprint Owner(SO): Hey Trent, what's up?
Me: So you know this position you said was worth 60 points? Has something changed?
SO: No, why? It's still the top priority to get filled.
Me: Does the hiring manager know it's your top priority?
SO: He better.
Me: Well, we've sent X number of qualified candidates, but he hasn't returned any calls, emails, or anything. I will move on to the next job on the priority list if that's ok with you.
SO: Give me 30 minutes.
-20 minutes later...
SO: You will hear from them in the next 5 minutes. If he doesn't get this role filled in this Sprint or the next one, it's going to be his ass, not yours! Deal?

That is the kind of partner you need to be successful in implementing Sprint Recruiting. Not all of our Sprint Owners are like that, but the ones who usually get priority on our team. Take your time to help develop the relationship needed with your sprint owner for both of you to be successful.

Stakeholders
A stakeholder is a broad term to identify key partners in the recruiting process. This could include your HR partners,

senior-level executives (not Sprint Owners but maybe their boss), operational support members, or anyone else who plays a role in the recruiting process. The stakeholder involvement will be driven primarily by how you define it. In the beginning, we involved our HR business partners in our standup and retro meetings. It sounded like a great idea until the team got too big for the meetings to be effective. Some recruiters scheduled weekly huddles with the HRBPs to provide critical updates on the Sprint's progress. Most HRBPs now join the client allocation and retro meetings as stakeholders, which have proven to be a more effective use of everyone's time.

Stakeholders can also include the top line business executive for the group you support. About half of our senior department managers have delegated the allocation of points and day-to-day sprint activities to a designated team member. Although they are not involved in the daily activities, we need to update our senior executives of the progress we make during the Sprint so we will have monthly stakeholder updates with them if needed or required. Believe it or not, many of these executives choose to review the sprint dashboards we have prepared and will schedule a meeting on an as-needed basis.

Stakeholders hold little power in the sprint process except for the senior business executive. Their role is to help provide perspective and support while primarily serving as the voice of the client. In the recruiting model, the voice of the client represents both hiring managers and candidates. I find stakeholders can help us identify potential risks or gaps in our processes quicker than we can, especially if we consider any change. They're our voice of reason and mediator throughout the Sprint.

Each role within the sprint recruiting model works together to attain the highest percentage of points won during the Sprint. When each person in the group functions under the roles and responsibilities outlined, you'll find the process moves smoother, and efficiencies found. There will be fewer disasters that surprise you because the Sprint recruiting model creates a cadence of communication to prevent such blunders.

Key Term: Definition of Done
In the Agile framework, a fundamental definition of what "Done" must be established. One of my favorite authors, Brene Brown, talks about the importance of a team definition when a project is complete. For her team, "paint done" creates space for input from all parties. It "unearths stealth expectations and unsaid intentions, and it gives the people charged with the task tons of color and context," she writes. "It fosters curiosity, learning, collaboration, reality-checking, and ultimately success."

Early in our beta version of Sprint recruiting, we decided to define Done as when the candidate started. It seemed like the most straightforward, easy way to determine when we were done with a job in the Sprint, but it presented some data obstacles we did not think through. Our goal was to track the candidate journey's improvement, but some aspects of the onboarding process were outside of our control. We decided to redefine our definition to circumvent these obstacles and reclassify our Done to mean when the candidate accepts and signs the offer letter.

It may not seem like an important step, but I will caution you that skipping this step can prove detrimental to your implementation. Done's definition will be what your team and the client use to stop the clock on the sprint process so take the time to think through what works best for your team.

Now that we've identified the key roles and terms for our Sprint recruiting model let's discuss each of the four principles that comprise the methodology. The following four chapters will discuss each principle in-depth and provide examples of how you and your team can quickly implement Sprint recruiting successfully to reach the recruiting utopia.

The Business Defines the Priority

The key is not to prioritize what's on your schedule but to schedule your priorities. Stephen Covey

Have you ever gone to the grocery store without a shopping list? Maybe it was just a quick run to the store for only four items, and you thought, surely you could remember four things, right? How many times have you walked out of the store, get home, only to realize the main reason you went to the store was to get the one item you forgot?

This is what happens when we don't have priorities. Our brains are wired to rank lists in terms of importance. Stop and think about it:
- 1st, 2nd & 3rd place
- Gold, Silver Bronze
- High, Medium, Low

Ranking allows the brain to assess which tasks should be completed first quickly. It provides structure to large sets of information and creates a virtual roadmap for items to be completed. Absent of a ranking system, our brains attempt to classify data into subsets for quicker processing. This process of prioritization taxes the brain and quickly causes fatigue and anxiety.

Before implementing Sprint Recruiting, I found it hard to balance what should be with what needed to be done. I felt I could prove to my clients I was Superman because I am an overachiever. The value drove the other part of me I placed on the relationships I had developed with my hiring managers. Both pushed me to succeed, but I did not have a straightforward way to chart my ultimate destination. What I needed to learn was how to set priorities in my recruiting process.
Imagine a job board with 25 positions, each with a different manager and a different required skill set. Each job is

essentially its unique search, which will require a specific investment of time and administrative work.
Which job do you start on first?

The tendency is to go after the low hanging fruit, the job with the most applicants. It'll be easier to sit and comb through a ton of resumes (most of which will not qualify) than it would be to tackle the more challenging jobs requiring sourcing. If this sounds familiar, don't beat yourself up because I'm guilty of doing the same. Sometimes we just need a quick win to get us going and prove to ourselves we can get through the monumental task of making all of our managers happy with perfect candidates.

Unfortunately, this is just one lie of traditional recruiting tempts is to believe.

It's the most misleading concept in business is the idea that multitasking and productivity are related. The more you multitask, the more you can get done, which means you're more productive. Many say the most valuable resource is time, but I am of the school of thought that focus is much more critical. (Just as an example-I've attempted to write this chapter at least seven times today but have stopped to take a call, answer an "urgent" email or handle some other form of the focus-sucking action item.) Many of us are constantly bombarded with interruptions that drain our focus, and we relinquish our ability to be truly effective in our job. This is commonly referred to as context switching.

There has been a lot of research about the effects of focus on the brain. Dr. Jim Taylor, Sports Psychologist and contributor for the Huff Post, suggests the focus is the gateway to business success:

Focus is important because it is the gateway to all thinking: perception, memory, learning, reasoning, problem-solving, and decision making. Without good focus, all aspects of your ability to think will suffer. Without focus, you won't be as effective in your work because if you're not concentrating on the right things or are distracted, you won't be capable of getting your work done.

One research group tested the hypothesis that making many choices impairs our self-control. A group of psychologists conducted four laboratory studies where participants made choices among consumer goods or college courses. The other group of participants in the study was given the same options, but they were not required to choose. The study found the group required to make choices experienced reduced self-control, reduced persistence when faced with failure, and a reduced ability to solve math calculations. This research explains why many recruiters who attempt to multitask are not as effective as those who focus on one to five jobs at a time. It's no wonder we are mentally exhausted by lunchtime.

I know reading the last statement, you are probably like, "duh," but think about your current requisition load. Is it more than ten? If so, did you spend most of the last week bouncing among jobs and not making a lot of progress? If so, you're experiencing a depletion of focus, which inevitably leads to a deficit of productivity.

To test the theory, I began trying different ways to focus as the first step in a productivity hack one month. I started using the time blocking method discussed in numerous books to chart my week. I reintroduced ToDoist in my routine to help dump those pesky items that come to mind to keep my focus and remain productive. At the end of the week, I used a weekly review to help me evaluate everything that went well during the week to find ways to scale these practices in the future. I also spent some time identifying what didn't work so I could create a plan to avoid these pitfalls the following week. The result? With only a minor tweak or two, I cut down on the noise of life and focus. Not only had I seen an increase in productivity, but I have also experienced a decline in mental exhaustion at the end of the day.

Let's apply the assumption that focus is a limited resource and multitasking does not equate to productivity. Traditional recruiting methods led us to believe we were ultra-productive when we were creating more work for ourselves. The constant starting and stopping increased errors and would often botch our dreams of a great candidate experience. Our continuous shift in focus created even more chaos in a process belabored by turmoil.

I wanted to discover a way to prioritize the team's worth in a way that was easy to implement and efficient. I struggled with this for weeks. I knew there had to be an answer, but I just could not figure out how to structure the prioritization correctly. I felt like the recruiting team, our clients, and our HR partners were all attempting to speak the same language, but it just entirely wasn't there yet.

I think it's important to share the journey with you to avoid some of the pain we experienced trying to find what method worked best.

First Iteration
Our first stab at this problem was to have our clients assign a High, Medium, or Low status to each job posted. This helped us at the beginning of the iteration focus on prioritizing our efforts. We used the high, medium, low assignments to break down how we would spend our time sourcing during the week. My approach was to dedicate the first 40 percent of my week to sourcing for those high priority positions to start getting candidates in the funnel early in the sprint. Once I felt ok with the number and quality of candidates in the process, I'd move on to my medium priorities to do the same.

At first, I felt like I had a process that was working. I had a cadence and system for my week. I knew every sprint would be front-loaded with sourcing time for those critical roles as defined by my client. I felt good knowing the clients' priorities were my priorities. Everything started to align perfectly for me.

I didn't plan for the major issue- just how many jobs would be categorized as a high priority. One client marked ten of their twenty jobs in a sprint as high and the remaining as a medium priority. I had no system put in place to limit the number of high-priority designations, so essentially, I had just added an H, M, or L next to our job board.

What was the issue?

We realized we were on to something. While it was not a slam dunk win, we made some slight advancement in this iteration. We did see an increase in focus and productivity during this iteration. The ranking helped us prioritize our tasks, and we began talking more as a team about our high priority positions during our standups.

What did we learn? We were one step closer to aligning our efforts to our clients' priorities. The problem?

The client still had too many priorities.

Second Iteration
We decided that we would limit the number of High, Medium, and Low priority assignments in our second iteration. Twenty-five percent of the open jobs could be High, another 25% could be Medium, and the remaining would be Low priority.

The first sprint we introduced was a little bumpy. The clients struggled while trying to determine a narrower definition of high and medium priority. Some asked for a bit of wiggle room on the percentages, but we held firm. Internally, we struggled as a team because we had all been programmed to fill every position as fast as possible. There were some instances when I almost caved on my own rules but reminded myself of limited capacity. I also reminded myself we were not superheroes, so we needed to stick with the plan.

The second iteration helped us focus even more on time, blocking for sourcing, interviewing, and our job's administrative functions. We even agreed that by day three of the sprint, we would send an update email to our managers with high priority positions informing them of our progress. With fewer high and medium priorities, we were able to use our sourcing time even more efficiently.

A couple of sprints into this iteration, we noticed how hard it was to report our progress. Did we report how many high, medium, low positions we filled or report a goal percentage? Many of our business partners who assigned the priorities would forget the positions' prioritization by the end of the sprint.

The progress we made in limiting the priority positions created some capacity and efficiency, but it did not truly measure our progress effectively. How could we prove to our clients and ourselves how well we were doing?

This was about the time I read the book SCRUM by Jeff Sutherland. One chapter dedicated to the development of stories identified a way to focus on the end-user. Points were applied to each story or epic to indicate priority and to measure progress in each sprint.

There it was. I am not exaggerating when I say I yelled, "Holy shit!" when I got to this part of the book. Finally, I saw what was right in front of me the whole time—no more high, medium, or low assignments. We were going to a point system! I was so excited to get to the office and share my vision for our third iteration with the team.

As a team, we agreed it would make sense to give each group a budget of points to assign to their roles during the sprint. We didn't put a lot of thought into the budget during that first brainstorming session. The very first client sprint call, we introduced the concept of 100 points as the budget. Not an example of how our team normally thinks through this, but this time it was gold. We worked through the first call with one of our clients who enjoy trying new things. They were as invested in making this new recruiting methodology work as much as we were. As we went through these group's

20 positions to assign points, we noticed something. We were all speaking the same language.

Rather than seven to ten high priority jobs out of a batch of 25 jobs, we had a clearer ranking of what was critical to the business. Our business partner gave one job 25 points, another two 15 points, and then spread the remaining points equally over the remaining roles. When we hung up the phone, the recruiter and I immediately began planning how we would get those two jobs filled to show the clients we were rock stars.

We almost became obsessed with the points. Our standups became centered around the progress we had made on high point roles. My one on one meetings focused on the progress made during the week on the "high pointers," which gave us a standard plan for this biweekly time together. We built dashboards to track how many points we gained by day during the sprint to chart our progress individually and as a team. Our clients liked it too. It was clearer for them to assign points against a budget.

We did make a minor tweak to point allocation in the middle of our third iteration, instituting a rule that our client spread 60% of the points over no more than five roles. Initially, this was a challenging concept for the client, but the clients began to see how the prioritization and focus produced results over time. If you have 100 points and have 25 jobs, it might be easy for the client to simply assign four points to each position initially. Fortunately, we had been through two iterations over roughly three months by the time we discovered the point system, so it was an easier transition for our clients.

The consistent progress we made in each sprint filling the jobs bought us more credibility and trust with our clients. It also allowed us to position ourselves less as order takers and more as consultants. During the biweekly allocation meetings, we would update the clients on progress made during the previous sprint while also identifying and addressing any obstacles.

The points allowed us to have a common language. Our clients were business people, and they're accustomed to numbers. We are recruiters and competitive by nature. Numbers worked. Metrics also helped us fine-tune our recruiting processes and jargon.

Finally, I felt like we were making progress!

How to implement the Point System

When we met with our client in the beta phase of Sprint Recruiting, our clients asked, "You want me to assign what?" They had become accustomed to the biweekly meeting to prioritize their work, but the use of points was new. It took a couple of iterations to find the best way to position the idea to our clients. Once they grasped the concept, it changed the way we communicated success.

There is no set number of points you must work with when you are starting the process. My team and I chose 100 points because we wanted to grade our performance each sprint like getting a grade in school. As we rolled this process out to other company areas, some organizational units were substantial. We gave each department head 100 points, which could mean the department could have 800 points available at the top of the house.

I would caution you to try to be consistent with each department's budget. If you have six departments in one division of your firm, give each the same amount of points so you can analyze the results comparatively. If one department has 100 and the other has 200, it will be hard for you to compare the sprint results. Remember, the points are to help you review which sprints are successful and those when we missed excitations. We'll discuss later how to chart your progress but be sure to remember this consistency rule.

For leaders, the point system also allows you to best understand which area of the company should have the most resources during a sprint. Maybe one of your department's number of open roles is trending higher and has a higher number of points. You will be able to divert recruiters to those jobs using the point system.

One trick we discovered during this process is front-loading sourcing help at the beginning of the sprint. If we had a department or division with a higher amount of points and no candidates, we would use others on the team who could dedicate themselves to sourcing or screening during the first two days of the sprint. Once they could help their team members progress toward their candidate goals, they would go back to their requisitions. Our team called this "swarming" around critical roles and was incredibly useful when faced with high profile openings.

Let's walk through an example:

Your client has 15 open positions at the beginning of the sprint. The budget for your sprint is 100 points. You will work with the Sprint Owner to prioritize each of the 15 open positions. The first sprint's natural tendency will be for the client to assign equal value to each role. That will not work because you're merely adding points to the flawed process known as traditional recruiting. During your allocation meeting (to be covered later in the book), your goal is to have your client allot 50 points to their top 2-3 positions and smaller points to the remaining. Each position is not required to have a point value. It's highly encouraged for you to have some roles without points. It will drive your focus to the most critical jobs for the next two weeks.

Now that you have your points recorded, you and/or your team will need to determine how to maximize the time and resources available in the sprint to attain the highest number of points. A best practice is to email those hiring managers in the sprint-those who have jobs with points. In this email, recruiters inform them they will focus on the opening for the next two weeks and outline expectations and deliverables. We found managers responded well to this practice, and most would block off time for interviews and feedback sessions. It was a game-changer for our managers and us.

Also, encourage your team to schedule time on Day 1 of the sprint to time block the rest of their week. (More to come on time blocking later in the book.) Let's say you have six jobs with points for this sprint. One of my jobs is worth 50 points, and you realize I have no one in the pipeline. This role will become my obsession, so you will use Day 1 to time block sourcing time. Initially, this will be a guessing game, but as you become more accustomed to the sprint process, you will be able to judge how much time you will need to source candidates for your roles. Once I have time allotted for the 50 pointers, I'll then review the next two in the priority list and do the same. This technique becomes invaluable and will increase your ability to meet the needs of your clients.

After our first couple of allocation meetings, the team and I had a very clear expectation of success, defined by our client every two weeks. We were able to finally plan our weeks and allocate the appropriate amount of time to source and fill those critical roles with the most points. Once we hit the Work in Progress limit for the various stages of the process (more to come on WIP limits), we moved on to the next highest pointed role in the sprint.

We discovered when we all slipped into the traditional methodology of filling everything, but the points system continuously increases our focus back to what matters in the sprint. To help maintain our focus, many of us kept our sprint charts up throughout the day as a reminder to refocus when we needed it.

After roughly 90 days, we began seeing the impact. Not only were we a bit more sane and organized, but the time to fill for priority roles also began decreasing. The focus on these roles in two-week sprints allowed us to move candidates quicker and created mutual accountability with our clients. If a role was given points for the sprint and the manager began ghosting us, we simply went to our client and asked if the position still needed priority. The client partner would usually reach out to the hiring manager quickly, and miraculously, the recruiting flow resumed with more efficiency.

One bonus of the point system was finally tracking our performance against how our client determined success. We were able to analyze sprint over sprint how we were progressing or failing. It enabled us to address some key obstacles our client created every sprint. When we had our biweekly meeting, our client discussions focussed on the analytics versus hearsay. If we missed the mark of achieving less than 60% of points attained, we discussed what obstacles prevented us from achieving our goal. The mutual accountability became evident early in the process. If the managers were slow to provide interview feedback, the numbers told the story. If a recruiter did not present enough qualified candidates, the numbers told the story. The point system allowed us to quantify how these obstacles affected the success of the sprint, creating some candid conversations and better relationships.

How do you handle unplanned critical roles?
Let's say you are on day 3 of your sprint, and your client calls you frantic because their top performer or most critical executive just turned in their notice. Do you tell the client, "Hey, sorry, you'll have to wait until the next sprint?" Of course not!

We had one particular client that always had an emergency. Every scenario was a "stop drop and roll, hair on fire" role that had to be filled. The business executive teams' seemed to get some type of adrenaline hit from running from emergency to emergency. Unfortunately, our team was getting sucked into the mess, killing our focus and performance.

Our team tried a couple of options in our initial iterations of this process. We tried the idea of reallocating points in the middle of a sprint but found this created a lot of inaccuracies in our tracking. We did try asking the client to wait until the next sprint, but that wasn't accomplishing our goal of creating a superior client experience. Our goal was to find a way to honor the methodology and meet the client's needs while also tracking how many times these "fires" occurred during the process.

After several blunders, we finally agreed that going forward, any critical role that needed expedited attention would be deemed EXPEDITED and receive 100 points above the sprint budget. We began to recognize the priority set by our client while also providing us the ability to track how quickly we could fill critical and unplanned roles while also tracking the occurrences.

Why was this important?

What you call these roles is entirely up to you. We chose EXPEDITED since we felt Chicken Little would be inappropriate (although accurate). Regardless of how you label these roles or projects, you must create guidelines and get buy-in from your Sprint Owner administering the points. One rule we put in place for one of our more high volume groups was that each region had the extra 100 EXPEDITED points at their disposal. Only the regional executive could use this dispensation. It helped our team stay out of the prioritization process and put some responsibility on the client to discern what was and was not an emergency role.

You can also decide not to make 100 points for your framework. We chose 100 points because if we filled the role during that sprint, we would track a spike in our sprint graphs to notate how often the events occurred. Remember, the Sprint Recruiting Methodology doesn't change but how you need to execute it for your business is up to you and your client.

Once we started tracking these Chicken Little drills (our nickname), it showed us a critical gap that needed to be addressed. It wasn't a gap in our recruiting process but a gap in our relationship with our HR partners and our client. In roughly 75% of the scenarios, someone knew the roles were about to be vacated, but no one communicated this with the team or me. Similarly, we were not proactively engaging with our HR partners and the client to ensure we could be ready for the upcoming departures of critical roles.

Tracking our sprint points and recognizing how many times expedited roles caused us stop as a team and evaluate. First, we strengthened our relationship with our clients through the biweekly retroactive and prioritization calls. We became even more entrenched in our business lines to stay abreast of potential issues before they happened. Second, we reorganized the work on our team to increase one team member's capacity to be able to be our firefighter. We agreed any time there was an unplanned, critical position in the sprint, it would go to our designated team member who would run with it and give it special attention. The result? Increased efficiency and a barrier to keep us from being sucked into the craziness of the fire drills.

Compare this process to traditional recruiting. In the old model, the ability to address the barrage of critical requests were low. As the manufacturing belt continued to speed up, we would have done everything and anything we could have to keep up. We would have sacrificed quality, efficiency, and our sanity. Sprint recruiting allowed us to stop, retool our approach, and our team to meet our clients' needs while protecting our efficiencies and sanity. It also allowed us to track the number of occurrences and leverage data to have a candid conversation with our client about prioritization.

What about roles without points?
We were close to a year in our sprint implementation throughout the firm when we finally tackled how we track progress on jobs without points? Until that point, we felt as though we were not reaching our actual ability to maximize the points won each sprint due to competing priorities. We tracked our points won versus points assigned and noticed specific sprints were significantly less than others. During one of our retro meetings, a team member discussed how they were busy filling jobs where candidates had been referred to or identified by hiring managers. These were easy fills that needed to be done but diverted a lot of focus from sourcing and filling our sprint roles.

The team and I debated a couple of ways we could track the activity on non-sprint roles. We decided to give points to these roles and designate them as "Extra Credit." We agreed we should find a way to track how often these activities kept us from meeting our sprint goals to quantify all of the work done in the sprint and coach our clients on the importance of prioritization during our allocation calls.

Let's look at an example of this in action. Let's say you have a client who has 10 jobs active for the sprint. In traditional recruiting, this is what your job board would most likely look like:

Job ID	Job Title	Manager
Req1234	Project Manager	John Smith
Req1235	Business Analyst	Jane Doe
Req1236	IT Coordinator	Mariah Carey
Req1238	Call Center Rep II	Will Smith
Req1239	Call Center Rep I	Will Smith
Req1240	IT Manager	J. Bourne
Req1241	IT Support Rep	Bon Jovi
Req1242	IT Analyst	Adam Levine
Req1237	Front Line Analyst	Brad Cooper

As a recruiter, what requisition do you start working on first? Do we know from this listing which roles are the most important roles to the organization? These are the typical questions left unanswered by Traditional Recruiting.

Now, let's apply our first principle of Sprint Recruiting to this scenario. You've given the Sprint Owner a budget of 100 points to allocate over the ten positions to dictate priority.

Once you've met with your client, they've decided to allocate the points shown in the table below:

Job ID	Job Title	Manager	Points Assigned
Req1234	Project Manager	John Smith	40
Req1235	Business Analyst	Jane Doe	20
Req1236	IT Coordinator	Mariah Carey	10
Req1238	Call Center Rep II	Will Smith	10
Req1239	Call Center Rep I	Will Smith	10
Req1240	IT Manager	J. Bourne	10
Req1241	IT Support Rep	Bon Jovi	
Req1242	IT Analyst	Adam Levine	
Req1237	Front Line Analyst	Brad Cooper	

We can quickly see that the Sprint Owner has identified John's role as the most critical in this sprint. The point system helps recruiters not only quickly prioritize the upcoming work but also align themselves to the needs of the client.

Remember, the use of points is how your client is going to define success over the sprint so be ready to push back. As we look at the allocation, we see a problem. Will Smith's roles are essentially the same, just different levels but both are allocated 10 points each. In this scenario, I would recommend one role be awarded 20 points since it's the same type of role. This will also allow you to leverage the extra credit function if you fill both roles. If we make this change, notice how the priority list changes.

Job ID	Job Title	Manager	Points Assigned
Req1234	Project Manager	John Smith	40
Req1235	Business Analyst	Jane Doe	20
Req1238	Call Center Rep II	Will Smith	20
Req1239	Call Center Rep I	Will Smith	
Req1236	IT Coordinator	Mariah Carey	10
Req1240	IT Manager	J. Bourne	10
Req1241	IT Support Rep	Bon Jovi	
Req1242	IT Analyst	Adam Levine	
Req1237	Front Line Analyst	Brad Cooper	

Now Will's roles are ahead of the IT Coordinator and IT manager roles and your team have the opportunity to fill two roles because of the focus placed on the top roles. This one step of adding points helped our team begin moving more efficiently and aligned with our client's needs. It added the level of prioritization we needed to properly plan our sourcing strategy for each sprint and measure our success. While this is a great first step, implementing Work in Progress Limits will add another level of efficiency your team will become addicted to.

Key Points The benefits of the point system in Sprint Recruiting:

- The business dictates the priority and creates mutual accountability
- The recruiter can focus on a batch of roles which will increase focus, efficiency while decreasing time to fill
- Points give you metrics to track what's working and what isn't

Work In Progress (WIP) Limits Drive Focus

One of the most iconic scenes from the show "I love Lucy" takes place in a candy factory. Lucy and her friend Ethel are assigned to the candy-dipping department, where they are trained for their role by a very strict and overly serious forewoman. The position seems relatively straightforward. Lucy and Ethel were to pick up a cream center, drop it into a bucket of chocolate, and make a swirl design on top. After a couple of failed attempts, Lucy finally manages to complete one and feels she has things under control...or so she thought.

At first, the candy comes through at a leisurely pace on a conveyor belt, and the two feel they have things under a bit of control. As the belt speeds up and the pieces double in volume, Lucy starts to put some of them next to her and gulps down others. When the belt stops, the two hear the forewoman coming, so they frantically gather up all the loose pieces, dropping them into their cook's caps. Scrutinizing their progress, she says, "Fine. You're doing splendidly. Speed it up a little!" she shouts. The speed and quantity of chocolate on the conveyor becomes so fast it overwhelms Lucy and Ethel. As the speed increases, they have a hard time keeping up and begin to stuff them down their blouses.

This hilarious scene is how I describe traditional recruiting. The quality of work Lucy and Ethel were able to accomplish diminished as the speed of the belt increased incrementally. There were no stop limits for the ladies to focus on the needed steps to adequately produce quality work. Traditional recruiting felt much like this iconic scene but without the laughter.

Let's reframe this scene to put it into a sprint recruiting model. In the scene, the product was "pushed" to Lucy and

Ethel without any worker having any control over the system's input. If limits were in place, Lucy and Ethel would have focused on the output quality before pulling the next cream filling into the system. The process's speed was dictated by the worker's ability to produce a product, not by the conveyor belt.

Lucy and Ethel would not have been so stressed and overwhelmed that they stuff candy into every nook and cranny they had available. With WIP limits, they would have had more control over the process and output. Once finished with one candy, they would move onto the next. Of course, there would be an increase in quality, increased production, and a decrease in stress and diverted focus.

When I attended a weeklong training on the Agile methodology and the Kanban process, I admittedly had some reservations that this training would be introducing me to more of a fad than a method. Over the last fifteen years, I've been a part of a lot of training on the "latest get productive quick" trends. Agile had become quite the buzzword in our firm, so I was anxious to see what all the fuss was about. This training was not anything like that!

One of the workshop activities was creating a paper boat making factory, which reminded me of the scene mentioned above. Each team member was responsible for one or two folds before passing it off to their partner to complete. The facilitators measured teams on how many boats were constructed and our waste at the end of the time allotted. Our first attempt was a little bumpy as each of us learned the process, but once we had our mojo, we felt that our paper boats' production was pretty stellar.

As my classmates and I were going through our iterations in our boat making activity, the facilitators stopped us. They instituted Work in Progress (WIP) limits for us to begin using. Each station was assigned a number, indicating the limit of boats that could be piled up. One person who had easy folds might have a WIP limit of ten, whereas the more complicated folds might have a WIP limit of five. Once a member's WIP limit was reached, the production process before that station stopped until we were below our WIPs. These limits helped us function better as a team and produce increased and better quality paper boats. It also reduced the stress we had experienced when chaos erupted in the previous scenario. Although it seemed counterintuitive at the time, putting limits on various stages of the process helped us exceed our goal.

The Agile methodology defines WIP limits as fixed constraints that individuals, teams, or organizations create to limit the total number of work items in the process at any given time. Instead of starting a new task when something becomes blocked or too difficult, WIP limits force teams to look at why a particular piece of work has not moved forward. Then focus on doing whatever is necessary to finish it so that more work can start to come in and so that the flow of work through the system can resume.

In sprint recruiting, WIP limits keep the process moving. Once you're at your limit for a role, you move on to the next one in priority. I've used the example of WIP limits serving like the beat in a song. Every beat keeps the process moving on to the next verse or measure. It's consistent and almost predictable, which allows the listener to focus on the story the song is telling. WIP limits are the beating drum that helps your team quickly evaluate what needs to be done on each role in a priority format.

WIP limits prevent team members from starting tasks on multiple requisitions at the same time. They help your team manage capacity, focus on critical tasks, identify opportunities for continuous improvement, and introduce previously unseen capacity in your process. So say goodbye to the chaotic candy factory and be ready for the new, recruiter controlled rhythmic approach aligned to client expectations but without all of the low-quality outputs, fire drills, and recruiter stress.

WIP limits enable us to manage capacity

Everyone has a finite amount of time, energy, and brainpower every day to maximize customer value. Unfortunately, most teams are unaware of how to manage their capacity effectively. The traditional recruiting approach is to maximize each individual's capacity on the team so that every team member can reach 100% utilization. It simply doesn't work.

If each team member is at 100% utilization on the requisitions they're assigned, it means they have no capacity for collaborating with their team, responding to questions, or helping each other deliver work across the finish line. In reality, 100% utilization means that everyone is impossibly busy — but nothing is getting done. It also means no one is reviewing how to work more efficiently, perpetuating the chaos, and lack of productivity.

WIP limits help to utilize the group effectively. Instead of a system where each person is trying to push their tasks to the next step, we create a system in which the team collaborates to move work from start to finish as quickly as possible. This includes recruiting team members and working with our clients to get candidates to the finish line.

WIP limits encourage us to practice systems thinking

WIP limits force us to work as a team to prioritize, plan, complete and deploy work. This practice is known as systems thinking – making decisions that benefit the entire team to contribute to achieving team goals. It allows recruiting leaders to move resources to the jobs with the highest value to the firm, busting through the traditional silos on most recruiting teams. Once we've identified members who can help, we realign them for the sprint, or even a couple of days during the sprint, to support front-load sourcing efforts to help meet our goals.

During your standup meeting, it's important to review the WIPs with the team to assess better who needs help. It is an opportunity to evaluate the team's current workload and

discuss how to move jobs off the board as efficiently as possible. Here are some examples:
- What's closest to being done? What can we do today to move it to "Done"?
- Is anyone working on anything that's not on sprint or doesn't have points assigned?
- Is anything currently blocked from making progress?
- Is anyone available to help move job X to "Done"?

Instead of asking, "What should I work on next?" WIP limits force us to ask, "What can I help move to *Done* before I begin working on another job?"

WIP limits help us identify opportunities for process improvement

When we're overburdened with too much WIP, we lose the bandwidth to observe and analyze our processes. The traditional recruiting model forces recruiters to do anything to get the work done without paying much attention to how they go about doing it.

Implementing WIP limits allows us to clarify our processes and whether they are working for us. In addition to enforcing WIP limits, many teams find it useful to implement clear process policies and hold each other accountable for following the team's guidelines. I've seen many team members work with each other to call out unnecessary steps to the process during our standup. They'll also offer up help in the form of advice or jumping in on a critical role to help source, screen candidates, or set up interviews. Once the WIP is met for the position, the helping team member will go back to their requisition board. This principle has proven invaluable for us during peak recruiting seasons.

Teams can work to identify patterns in things like bottlenecks, blockers, handoff delays, etc. They can discuss these patterns and hold periodic retrospectives to discuss and implement improvements to their processes.

WIP limits introduce slack into the system

Introducing WIP limits means that some team members will be underutilized or "have the capacity." The underutilized time referred to as slack, can be viewed as a healthy system sign in sprint recruiting. Slack time creates space for improving the way we work. Team members can use the slack time to implement continuous improvement efforts, watch educational webinars, or brainstorm ideas to optimize recurring programs. As mentioned above, they can jump in and help struggling team members or work on a unique project to create future efficiencies in our process. This benefits the group and allows recruiters to avoid the burnout commonly experienced in traditional recruiting.

Slack time is an incredible opportunity for professional development during work hours and can contribute significantly to job satisfaction. WIP limits enable us to slow down and work intentionally to create space for growth.

Learning to limit work in process can be challenging because WIP limits force us to have the discipline to say "no" when we're accustomed to saying "yes." They encourage us to abandon the frantic, chaotic way of working that we've come to define as "productivity."

They expose our bad habits and hold us accountable to the work of not just ourselves but our team. Over time, you'll begin to see the method to this madness: You'll get more done with less resistance and stress. You'll rediscover the power of effective collaboration. Your team will operate with a synergy that you may not have ever thought possible. You'll regain the luxuries of focus, creativity, and clarity, which will allow you to engage with your work in a more fulfilling way.

At the beginning of your implementation, especially for a team without much Agile experience, it can be tricky to set an appropriate WIP limit. Make the limit too strict initially, and people will get discouraged, frustrated, or even worried. If you set the limit too high, you will be able to work on too many things at once, which will, in turn, defeat the whole purpose of having a WIP limit in the first place.

If you think about any recruiting process, it comes down to three lanes or stages:
1. Recruiter Screening/Interviewing
2. Hiring Manager submissions
3. Hiring Manager interviewing

Your team should pick initial limits they feel comfortable with and can commit to following for at least two sprints. After two sprints, you and your team should properly evaluate if your WIPs need any adjustments. Discuss feedback during your retrospective session to decide as a team the limits going forward. As the team matures, the WIP limits should get smaller. Ideally, the WIP limit for everyone should be three to five, but that can sometimes be unrealistic. Please rely on the team to use their best judgment and find the best solution for the team as a whole or by an individual group.

Establishing the WIPs for your organization will take some trial and error. Our first step was charting the candidate's journey. We wanted to measure the number of days a candidate spent in each stage of our process. Most applicant tracking systems will track the date the candidate placed into each step of the process. Explaining the process might be confusing so let me share our approach in a more formulaic form below.

- **Recruiter Screening/Interviewing**: Date Applied until Date the recruiter interviewed
- **Hiring Manager submissions**: Hiring Manager Submitted the Resume until the Hiring Manager Disqualified or Interviewed
- **Hiring Manager interviewing**: Date Submitted for Hiring Manager Interview until Date Disqualified or Offered

The results were depressing.

We found two considerable bottlenecks in our process when we graphed out our candidates' journey. The first bottleneck was when a recruiter was screening a candidate and submitting them to the hiring manager. The second was the period between hiring managers interviewing and deciding on the final candidate. Throughout this process, we noticed how many candidates got lost or disenfranchised during the process. We discovered this was a significant opportunity for us.

We ran some tests on each stage to determine what the WIP limits should be. We had some recruiters who did high volume recruiting and others who worked on more mid to executive-level jobs. There was a lot of debate around whether there should be different WIPs for high volume roles. We tested this theory but found that establishing the same WIP limit across the team was easier to monitor. There was a minimal variance between the two volumes of recruiting.

Recruiter Screening/Interviewing Swim lane
The first step of the process is understanding how many candidates recruiters can manage without letting candidates fall through the gaps. We broke this swim lane into two parts: recruiter reviewing or sourcing the resume and recruiter interviewing the candidate.

The first phase of our process was reviewing candidates who had applied to determine who was qualified. It also included candidates we had identified during our sourcing efforts, which we were attempting to lure into the interview process. These two phases could work concurrently in any search, which allowed us to identify the top candidates to get to our hiring managers.

We defined the interview process separately because we wanted to have a place to stop and evaluate which candidates were the most qualified for the position. This was an early improvement in our process. We found ourselves finely tuning our sourcing efforts to bring the best candidates to the table early in the process.

After a couple of weeks of testing, we arrived at a WIP limit of ten for this stage. Some recruiters broke this into 5 in the reviewed or holding phase and 5 in the interview phase.

Others on our team just worked to make sure they had ten qualified candidates in the process to keep their candidate funnel full.

Your organization will have to go through the same testing process to find what the WIP limit works best for you in this phase. I would encourage you to test a couple of limits to find what works best for you and be aware that it might make sense for different recruiting groups to have different WIPs.

Hiring Manager Submitted

Once the recruiter screens and interviews the candidate, they typically submit them to the manager for feedback. We set the bar high initially at ten candidates in this stage but quickly discovered that there were too many. Managers were either complaining that we were sending too many candidates or complaining they didn't have enough time to review the candidates, creating over analysis paralysis.

Once we decided the WIP for this group was five, we began seeing a lot of progress. Managers could manage to work through five candidates relatively quickly. We started seeing quicker response times and better feedback to help us strengthen our sourcing strategy.

Hiring Manager Interview

During our candidate journey analysis, we noticed one manager had twenty candidates in the interview process either via phone or in person. The in-person interviews consisted of six people in different locations, which required working across multiple time zones and booking multiple rooms with video conference capabilities. This was a drain on our process that we immediately fixed by limiting the number of candidates in the interview process.

We decided to learn from our previous test and set the WIP at five. We determined if managers became easily overwhelmed with five submissions, they'd be even more overwhelmed with more than five interviews in the process. Recruiters also noticed how overwhelming it was to schedule more than five in-person interviews at a time. Between the continually moving calendars for both the managers and the candidates and the number of rescheduling requests we typically got during this process, it began to make sense why this was one of our significant bottlenecks.

When you introduce this concept to your hiring managers, be prepared for some resistance. We found this part of the process a major pain point as we introduced sprint recruiting to our clients. If you get too much pushback, increase your WIP, and measure the lack of efficiency to show your clients the difference a lower WIP can bring them.

WIP Guidelines

With your WIP limits determined, you're now ready to put the process in motion.

The best way to see WIP in action is to create a visual tool to track how many candidates you have in each stage of the process. Some applicant tracking systems will do this for you, but I have found very few as useful as creating a Kanban board.

A Kanban board is an Agile project management tool designed to help visualize work, limit work-in-progress, and maximize efficiency (or flow). Kanban boards use cards, columns, continuous improvement to support technology, and service teams commit to the right amount of work and get it done!

David Anderson established that Kanban boards could be broken down into five components: Visual signals, columns, work-in-progress limits, a commitment point, and a delivery point. This is an excellent definition for software development, but for Sprint Recruiting, we only need four:
1. Recruiting Sourcing/Interview,
2. Hiring Manager Submitted,
3. Hiring Manager Interview, and
4. Done.

Most ATS platforms are severely lacking in the ability to set up a Kanban-style board. When we were first testing Spring

Recruiting, we were using ICIMs as our ATS. The company was incredible to work with and formatted our version to replicate a Kanban board. The team knew their WIP limits, and it was easy to keep track of how many candidates were in each stage of the process. We've since moved from ICIMs, and I hate to say that we lost this valuable feature. Our team uses a massive Google Sheet to track our candidate flow, which is helpful but not ideal.

Once you have your preferred Kanban tool, it's time to get to work. (I'll discuss some options in the chapter on metrics later in the book.) Begin holding your team accountable for staying within their WIPs early in your beta process. This tool helps them retrain their brain to avoid slipping back into the traditional recruiting mindset. It is perhaps the most challenging part for recruiters to get accustomed. Help them avoid the lure of being busy over being productive.

Recruiters reach the WIP in each stage, stop working on the position and move to the next with the highest number of points. The only way to get more candidates to be reviewed and/or interviewed, the manager has to provide feedback on candidates presented. It keeps the recruiting process moving efficiently and minimizes any loss in focus from the recruiting team.

At this point, let's show how the first two principles work together to illustrate the importance of WIP limits better. I've found this concept is easier to understand when seen in action versus only discussing it in theory. We'll use the example from the previous chapter to show how prioritization and WIPs work together. One of your new behaviors will be planning your work and capacity at the beginning of each sprint, so prioritizing and WIP limits will prove critical to this new behavior's success. First, let's talk about time blocking as a new behavior to help you maximize the benefits of prioritization and WIP Limits.

The Importance of Time Blocking
"A 40-hour time-blocked work week, I estimate, produces the same amount of output as a 60+ hour work week

pursued without structure." – Cal Newport, author of Deep Work.

Another critical component to discuss is the importance of time blocking to maximize efficiency. I've become a firm believer in controlling my calendar rather than allowing it to control me. Time blocking is a simple way to plan time sections to block out to complete essential work. For recruiters, time blocks are often used to designate time to source and screen candidates, handle administrative work, and work on recruiting strategy.

According to the Todoist Blog (one of my favorite tools), time blocking is incredibly helpful if you:
- Juggle many different projects/responsibilities (Jack Dorsey uses day theming to run two major companies at the same time)
- Spend too much time in "reactive mode," responding to email and messages
- Find their day chopped up by meetings
- Battle constant interruptions throughout the day
- Struggle to find the time and mental space for big-picture thinking

The goal of time blocking is to divide your day into blocks of time dedicated to accomplishing a specific task or group of functions, and only those particular tasks. Most recruiters like to have an endless to-do list of things they hope to get done during the day. When you use the time blocking mindset, you'll begin each day with a focused schedule that outlines not only what you'll work on but also when.

There is absolute freedom that comes from doing this method correctly. I sometimes struggle focusing on key drivers of success during the day because my thoughts drift in and out of the endless list of demands. Now that I use time blocking when those thoughts creep in, I stop, add it to the most appropriate time block, and get back to my tasks at hand. The freedom to scratch the itch but categorize and forget it has allowed me to end my days feeling less stressed, more accomplished, and more efficient. I noticed when days are time blocked in advance, and I don't spend time worrying about what I need to focus on or accomplish.

Todoist gives some great advice on how to begin this behavior:

> *The key to this method is prioritizing your task list in advance – a dedicated weekly review is necessary. Take stock of what's coming up for the week ahead and make a rough sketch of your time blocks for each day. At the end of every workday, review any tasks you didn't finish – as well as any new tasks that have come in – and adjust your time blocks for the rest of the week accordingly.*

Teaching my team to time block was a different story. The idea of turning off your email and chat to focus on sourcing for a critical role sounded like a great idea until recruiters had to execute it. I think the biggest mistake most of us made involved committing two to three hours to source or work on a project. We committed to "going off the grid" (email, chat, etc.) to focus, but I think the longest most of us lasted was roughly 45 minutes. I'd encourage you and your team to start with 30-minute increments and build up the skill before going all in.

Another version of time blocking is to have "theme days." Maybe Mondays and Fridays are your administrative days while Tuesday-Thursday is sourcing, screening, and offer negotiations. Dedicating each day to a single theme creates a reliable pattern of work and further limits the cognitive load of context switching, which leads to a loss of efficiency.
Let's say you're planning your week on the previous Friday afternoon or Sunday afternoon. Your first task is to jot down your goals for the week.

Let's look at an example:
1. Source for ABC Role and book 5 qualified interviews with the hiring manager.
2. Review applicants for my open roles and schedule phone screens for the week.

3. Conduct candidate screenings and prepare write-ups for the hiring managers.
4. Follow up with managers who interviewed candidates last week.
5. Research and create an outline for the presentation to executive management at the end of the month.

Once you have your goals for the week, you want to time block your week to make sure you progress on each of these goals. Remember, some of these most likely have 10+ sub-tasks below them. Thinking about all of the sub-tasks is what will overwhelm your brain and create chaos. The trick is to mentally dump those tasks into their time slot and move on. Each task completed will move you closer to accomplishing your goal. It helps you take the large daunting tasks of managing through your five goals and 100+ tasks and breaks them into small, manageable steps you can take every hour of every day.

Here's how I structure my days to accomplish maximum productivity as a recruiting leader. Below is my time blocking for every Tuesday through Thursday.

Time Block	Task
8:00 am	Administrative and follow up needs from yesterday
9:00 am	Daily stand-ups with the teams
10:00 am	Sourcing for critical roles in the sprint
2:00 pm	Follow up with managers who've interviewed candidates to get feedback
3:00 pm	Schedule interviews and follow up with candidates in the process
4:00 pm	Administrative tasks, project work/updates, planning for the following day

As I think of tasks during the day, I assign them to the appropriate time block. If I need to call candidate John Smith about scheduling an interview, I'll add it to my time block list for the 3-4 pm section designated for such tasks. If I have an excellent idea for a project I am working on, I'll add it to the deck to think through from 4-5 pm. Before blocking, I would get diverted chasing all of these random thoughts, but now, I have a time slot designated to capture them and give each task the proper amount of time to focus.

The most significant benefit I get from time blocking is the ability to do deep work. I am responsible for recruiting the critical roles for my firm and our recruiting strategy's continuous transformation to be one step ahead of our competition. Before time blocking, I rarely had time dedicated to deep work, and my output suffered accordingly. The more you "single-task," the more you build the mental muscles required for deep work, and the easier it becomes to stay focused.

Another key benefit is the ability to knock out shallow work or administrative tasks quicker. This type of work doesn't require a ton of mental resources, but it can tax the brain and increase the chances of mistakes if spread over the entire day. I noticed my ability to group similar tasks within the time block improved my ability to knock them off the to-do lists. Dedicating a daily block of time allows recruiters to complete the necessary, sometimes mundane parts of our job and reserve energy, focus, and creativity for the more value-add type of tasks.

A byproduct of this method is the retraining of your brain. Not only will you begin to categorize and assign tasks or ideas to their appropriate time block, but you will also start noticing how you spend your time. You may begin finding more efficient ways to block your week to maximize productivity. I already shared how Mondays and Fridays are often blocked off. I use those days for one on one meetings with my team, project work and meetings, and any other type of administrative work I may have for the week. This system works best for me, and I only found it after working in a time block for a couple of weeks.

Finally, as I became more comfortable and dependent on my time blocking routine, I noticed how I instinctively tied every idea or task to a goal. Although I follow the schedule shared above, I sometimes have overarching themed days dedicated to a project or goal.

Time blocking is a great tool, but you may wonder when you'll have the time to plan your activities. This is one of the critical benefits of prioritization and WIP limits. They allow you to quickly review your workload and identify how to organize your sprint to be successful. Let's look at our job board that includes the number of candidates in each stage of the process from our previous example.

Job ID	Job Title	Manager	Points Assigned	# of Candidates with Recruiter	# Of Candidates Submitted	# of Candidates in Interview with HM
Req1234	Project Manager	John Smith	40	3	3	5
Req1235	Business Analyst	Jane Doe	20	0	2	1
Req1238	Call Center Rep II	Will Smith	20	5	5	5
Req1239	Call Center Rep I	Will Smith				
Req1236	IT Coordinator	Mariah Carey	10	1	1	0
Req1240	IT Manager	J. Bourne	10	2	2	0
Req1241	IT Support Rep	Bon Jovi		5	5	5
Req1242	IT Analyst	Adam Levine		2	4	4
Req1237	Front Line Analyst	Brad Cooper		4	3	3

The first step of Sprint Recruiting is prioritization but adding the swim lanes to show the number of candidates in each stage of the process adds another level to consider. Let's assume the WIP limit for each swim lane is 5 candidates meaning your goal is to reach the max of 5 candidates in the Hiring Manager interview phase for this exercise.

Let's start with our priority role of 40 points for John Smith. At the beginning of the sprint, you would use this dashboard to determine what needs to be done to move this position to the Done stage so you can begin working on the next priority. John's role shows we have reached our WIP limit with 5 candidates interviewing with the manager. Although we've reached the WIP limit for the final swim lane, we do have the capacity in the number of candidates submitted for him to review if the 5 he is interviewing do not meet his needs.

We can see that we have interviewed 3 candidates we have not submitted to him to review. For John's priority role, the only tasks for the recruiter to complete would be first to identify the top two candidates they've interviewed and not submitted to be reviewed. The secondary task would be to schedule a quick call with John to gather feedback on the interviews completed and the candidates presented. It's an excellent habit to inform the hiring manager that you've reached your WIP limit and are moving on to the next role in priority until you receive feedback on the candidates in the process.

Now that we have our big pointer at the WIP limit, we move on to Jane Doe's role. If I'm reviewing our candidate lanes for this role, I would be a little worried as a recruiter. I have no one in my back pocket to interview and only have one in the interview stage and two awaiting feedback after I've submitted them. In this scenario, I'd probably make it a point early in the sprint to check in with Jane to see if I am on track and block some of my week to do additional sourcing and screening. I would not move on to other roles until I felt confident I was in a spot where I could hit my WIP limits for Jane within 48 hours.

I hope you can understand the difference between Traditional and Sprint recruiting. My tendency in traditional recruiting would have been to move on to identify some quick-hit roles like the ones for Bon Jovi, where I have a lot of candidates and can make a quick hire. While this is not necessarily a bad idea, the client has used their points to focus my attention on John's role, which is more important to them than Bon Jovi's. My behaviors and focus align with the client, and I can plan my week accordingly.

Notice how quickly this process takes when we have the prioritization and our WIP limits in view. Every day can begin with a recruiter quickly reviewing progress made the day before and charting their course for success. I don't have to wonder where I am in the process or which positions should be filled quickly. The data tells me what I need to know, and now I have to act on it.

Let's look at Will Smith's roles. I would want to get feedback from Will on the process early in the sprint since we're at our WIP limit. If he avoids my calls or is slow to respond, this is the perfect time for me to engage our Sprint Owner in the process. They've identified this is a key role to fill during the sprint and can leverage their influence to light a fire under Will to respond. There is a motivation for the Sprint Owner to work with me to ensure every role assigned points is closed because they're equally as responsible for the sprint's success. If I called a sprint owner to inform them I've been waiting beyond the agreed-upon time for feedback on ten qualified candidates, the hiring manager would promptly receive a call from the sprint owner and have a lot of explaining to do.

The beauty of the process is that it provides mutual accountability and enforces a team effort to fill the critical roles. The ability for recruiters to quickly assess their progress and identify where their focus should create an addictive level of efficiency in the process. While WIP limits take a bit of adjustment, the benefits far outweigh the mindset shift you and your client will endure as you adapt to Sprint Recruiting.

WIP Limit Guidelines to Remember

1. There's no formula but your own. There is no concrete mathematical formula for the ideal number of candidates to be working on at once. Test and determine which limits work for you and your team.
2. Adjust when necessary. Every organization experiences change at some point. When that happens, don't cling to your previous habits! Keep an eye on the flow of candidates and, if flow slows and bottlenecks appear, adjust your process, WIP included.
3. Don't break your rules! Do not break your WIP limits under any circumstances. If you break your limits even one time, you reduce the authority of this powerful control. This is one of the strengths of using WIP — it exposes flaws and previously hidden costs in the system.
4. Limit your Expedited roles. Limiting WIP of the "Expedited" lane to just one (a common practice) tells stakeholders you don't accept more than one urgent task at a time.
5. Measure lead times. You can track WIP limit success by measuring the number of days your candidates spend in each phase of the process. Shortening this time will be the efficiency measurement you will use to fine-tune your WIPs.

The Sprint Provides Efficiency

Everyone has an obsession in life, and one of mine is my health. Sure, I like to focus on my health to have a better life, but it's driven more by my desire to look good. I admit that I suffer from vanity.

I began my health journey in 2012 after realizing I had gained sixty pounds of fat and was pretty miserable. I have tried all kinds of fad diets, eating styles, and workout styles. Part of my research led me to High-Intensity Interval Training as a way to drop fat quicker. I was more interested in the promise to lose fat than I was in the workout. One of the workouts I tried included the use of sprints during runs. The idea was to alternate sprinting and walking during a set time to increase the bursts' heart rate. The first time I tried it, I wouldn't say I liked it, but it was better than spending forty-five minutes on a treadmill going nowhere.

Doing the HIIT training for thirty days was probably the most miserable health decision I made, but the results were incredible. I dropped ten pounds and experienced increased focus and determination. Of course, the nerd in me wondered whether this was a fluke or if there was actual science behind it.

The National Council on Strength and Fitness released an article encouraging trainers to consider sprint training to help clients meet their goals. It goes on to say that studies on sprinters showed less muscle decline than those athletes who only did the traditional form of working out, resistance training. During sprint training, the heart works very hard to meet the exercise's success's energy demands. By utilizing short duration, sprint-type activities, the strength of the heart will improve. At the muscular level, most individuals will not experience the same adaptations generally associated with aerobic training. The studies quoted showed more calories are burned during sprint training than anaerobic exercise.

One thing I found that helped me push through HIIT was the duration. Unlike trying to convince me to stay on a treadmill for forty-five minutes or run four miles, the HIIT routines were short but intense. I could mentally break the thirty-minute habit into, "OK, I'm going to do this exercise for the next five minutes."

For me, it was easier to get through those sprints than it was being bored with traditional cardio. I could do a burst of speed and then slow the pace to catch my breath and lower my heart rate. The HIIT workout's cyclical nature allowed me to think during those times and evaluate how I performed in the last exercise.

I began to use the rest to challenge myself. Could I make the next sprint with five-pound weights to make it a little more challenging? Maybe I could incorporate another movement in the sprint to engage another muscle group. What if I added ten pushups at the end of the sprint? Those thoughts NEVER crossed my mind while I was running for thirty minutes on a treadmill. HIIT broke up the thirty-minute cardio sessions into phases I could focus on and endure. Instead of looking down at the treadmill monitors to see I had only been running five minutes when my body felt like it had been an hour, I could pep talk myself into thinking, "Ok, I can do this one cardio exercise for another five-minute burst."

The same lessons I learned from my experience trying HIIT apply to sprint recruiting. Defining the sprint helps relieve the constant pressure I once felt looking at all of the open jobs our team had to fill. The goal was to move the needle in critical ways over two weeks. I focused more on how to win the play, knowing that when I won enough plays, I would win the game. The most significant improvement in sprint recruiting I experienced was the decreased times my brain entered shut-down mode. It was less of a mental drain to focus on five to ten jobs over two weeks versus forty jobs over one month. I found better candidates and had the time to be the talent consultant I was meant to be.

Another example of leveraging the sprint mentality is Nathan's Coney Island Hot Dog Eating Contest, an annual attraction on the 4th of July. The event attracts both competitors and audiences from around the world. Mountains of hot dogs are stacked in front of the competitors as the anxious crowds wait to cheer their favorite competitor.

Takeru Kobayashi, a small framed native of Japan, holds six Guinness Records for eating hot dogs, meatballs, and other junk food items. In 2001, he set his first record eating 50 hot dogs in 12 minutes at the Nathan's Coney Island Hot Dog Eating Contest. The secret to Takeru's success is his unique strategy to tackle monumental eating challenges by taking one bite at a time. Where many cringe and crack under pressure, Takeru continues to set world records with ease.

Takeru realized early in his competitive eating career that the biggest challenge is not the number of hot dogs but the tendency for people to have mental barriers. He sets a goal and works toward it methodically.

When asked about his ability to think without limits, Takeru said, "I think the thing about human beings is that they make a limit in their mind of what their potential is." Unlike Takeru, you may find that members of your team have preconceived limits that hold them back.

So as a recruiting manager, how do you help your team manage through times when they feel they have bitten off more than they can chew?

There's an old saying that the best way to eat an elephant is one bite at a time. Helping your team recognize that every project has bite-size pieces can be an excellent first step. Managing these smaller sized portions is an easy way to be able to avoid being overwhelmed.

As stress mounts, we tend to focus on the problem's enormity rather than the more manageable solutions. Team members who appear to be overwhelmed need you to coach them on finding the most practical strategy to complete their work. The real barrier may be all in their perception, and an objective viewpoint could be the perfect diagnosis of this common problem. Sprints break large recruiting workloads into two week periods of focus. The sprints have helped my team and our clients focus on what can be accomplished during this defined timeline, allowing us to achieve success more often. The sprints also enable teams to test new ideas or tactics in iterations to learn what works and what doesn't.

Without sprints, recruiters tend to work aimlessly on whatever position is the easiest to fill or the position with the noisiest client. It is a detriment to both the client and the recruiter.

Recruiting for multiple positions at a time can be an overwhelming task. You can use Takeru as an inspiration and teach them that the most significant barrier to success is a mental one that can be changed with the right perspective. Using sprints can help you accomplish your goals without cracking under pressure. It will enhance organizational productivity and show your client that you are committed to making them successful.

Definition of Sprint

A sprint is defined as a short, time-boxed period when a scrum team works to complete a set amount of work. Sprints are at the very heart of scrum and Agile methodologies, and getting sprints right will help your Agile team ship better software with fewer headaches.

> *"With Scrum, a product is built in a series of iterations known as sprints that break down big, complex projects into bite-sized pieces," said Megan Cook, Group Product Manager for Jira Software at Atlassian.*

Agile also uses the pull versus pull methodology to create efficiency. The push/pull terminology is commonly associated with logistics or operations management. Neither process is more right than the other, but we employ the pull method in sprint recruiting.

Imagine a factory with a line of workers assembling a product. Every time one station gets through with their portion of the assembly, they push it to the next and begin the process again. It's not a flawed method necessarily, but it takes longer for a push-based supply chain to respond to changes in demand, which can result in overstocking or bottlenecks and delays. It creates a ton of inefficiency in the process, which directly affects your profit line.

Imagine the same scenario, but this time, your station only begins working on a new assembly once your partnering station pulls your completed product to theirs. This is the pull method where production and distribution are demand-driven rather than a forecast.

To demonstrate the power of sprint in increasing efficiency, I usually have groups go through my "Paper Airplane Factory" session. The teams typically laugh and ask how hard making airplanes can be, but they learn how complicated it can be once they get into the process.

I recently conducted this training in Texas with my team members who were new to the sprint process. The exercise's goal is pretty simple- each completed airplane is a profit of $100, and they will have five minutes to see how many they can make. Each team member has one to two tasks to complete in the construction of the plane. Once completed, they are to move on to produce as many as they can in the allotted time. At the end of the session, we will measure profitability, waste, and backlogs. We would also break down their profit by minute to create our baseline to compare with future sessions.

There are usually three iterations in this training I like to use.
- **No Sprint:** It's relatively straightforward in this session. I time the group to see how many airplanes they can make using the push method.

- **1 Sprint**: We will stop the clocks at the middle mark to allow the team to assess what's working and what isn't to make necessary adjustments. In this iteration, the team has to use the pull method. This iteration begins to eliminate bottlenecks and reduces waste as the group starts to find a more productive rhythm.
- **2 Sprints** -We stop every minute and a half for 30 seconds to make changes and continue. Nothing is off the table. The teams are allowed to completely redesign the process in any way they feel to be more efficient. In this iteration, we also institute the WIP limits for each stage of the process.

I always enjoy facilitating this session and watching the teams work to streamline or enhance their process. I've seen multiple variations of this exercise, and no two methods have been alike. The power of sprints is the iterative learning gained by teams.

As an example, let's review the results of the Texas team.

Iteration 1: Push Method
- 10 planes completed
- Average of 3.33 planes per minute
- Total profit of $1,000
- Profit per minute of $333.33

Iteration 2: With 1 Sprint Iteration
- 13 planes completed
- Average of 4.33 planes per minute
- Total profit of $1,300
- Profit per minute of $433.33

Iteration 3: With 3 Sprint Iterations and WIP Limits
- 19 planes completed
- Average of 6.33 planes per minute
- Total profit of $1,900
- Profit per minute of $633.33

In the above example, profitability increased 200 dollars per minute or 90% from the first to third iteration. Only having one sprint iteration increased the profitability per minute by 30%. Without production teams' ability to stop, evaluate, and decide on better processes, the team would not have discovered additional efficiencies.

The idea of stopping in the middle of the process to discuss ways to increase production or deliberate on what method works better sounds counterintuitive to the participants at first. Once I show them the difference in the profitability per minute, they are almost always astounded by the increase in production and profitability. The 2nd and 3rd iterations are examples of how breaking a project into smaller time frames can increase productivity and efficiency.

Recruiting can be a rat wheel at times...well, most of the time. The sprints help leaders and their teams stop bi-weekly to discuss successes to find ways to scale them for future sprints. It could be a new sourcing tool, a new trick in your applicant tracking system that helped you bank more points. Regardless of the success, document these successes to implement and continue to evolve. Before Sprint Recruiting, this success sharing was limited. We usually continued doing the same old thing, the same old way, expecting better results week over week. Our Sprint Recruiting method has allowed us to formalize this sharing to maximize our iterative growth every two weeks.

The same is valid for identifying and discussing what went wrong. What are the obstacles? Is it a process or people? How do we overcome or avoid it next sprint? This process helps us not only scale our good but deal with our bad! (Sorry for the Facts of Life allusion!)
Similar to the airplane making exercise, our team has become better with each sprint. Sure, we still have some sprints when we wonder what the hell went wrong, but those have become fewer over time. We've also become closer as a team because we pause to celebrate our wins. It is vital in any recruiting but especially in corporate, in-house recruiting. Unlike working for a firm, we do not have the big "pay-day" celebration for big wins.

To begin, you'll first need to identify a business unit that is open to innovation. Our first couple of clients who were in our beta version of Sprint Recruiting were great partners not only because they embraced innovation but also because they gave great feedback. You will want to design your sprint around your client's needs, so it's critically important to have a reliable partner who will tell you the good and the bad as you begin your journey.

Second, you'll want to select the jobs to be included in the sprint. The easiest way is to have the entire business unit's roles in the sprint, but that may not always be the best scenario your first time into it. Talk with your client to garner their engagement in which method works best for them. Maybe you focus on particular job groups or families for your test sprint. Some firms I've worked with have decided to test sprint recruiting on high-profile projects, sourcing and hiring specific competencies like software development or project managers. The decision is yours but be sure to follow the "good partner selection" advice I mentioned earlier. That is the key to success.

Finally, you'll need to develop a point target to strive towards in your sprint. Your unrealistic instinct will be to achieve 100% but be realistic. We've been using sprint recruiting for close to two years at the time I'm writing this. Our goal for the high volume recruiting groups is to be above a 60% threshold each sprint. For our professional division, the goal is drastically different, with a baseline of 45%. These roles are more complicated, and there is a longer sourcing time so setting a 60% target is incredibly unrealistic.

During your testing, I would recommend starting low 40s as a target. The first two sprints will be bumpy as both you and your client work together to iron out some of the details. Give yourself and your team the latitude to set a low bar of success. Just remember not to be too discouraged during your first two or three sprints. The goal is to get everyone comfortable with breaking up the enormous task into two week periods. My experience has been that the third and fourth sprints usually begin an upward trajectory in your baseline.

The adage, "it's not a sprint; it's a marathon," is useful in some situations, but not when you want to increase efficiency in recruiting. A sprint is a powerful tool used to help drive innovation, bust down obstacles, and drive client experience. If you find yourself struggling and in a rut, give Sprint Recruiting a test drive with recruiting in sprints. It doesn't have to be a two-week sprint; maybe start with a four-week sprint.
Find what works for you, and keep iterating! I think you'll become addicted to the quick successes you'll achieve as a team.

Steps to implement your sprint

Designing your sprint is a critical step in the process. You and your team should meet to discuss each of the items below to determine what will work best for your team and the organization. The sprint is key to sprint recruiting efficiency, so be sure to take the needed amount of time to plan appropriately and set yourself up for success.

Define the length of your Sprint

There is no definitive time frame defining a sprint. My team decided two weeks was a reasonable period of time, and it broke our year up into 25 sprints. (We count the last two weeks of the year as a wash considering vacation times for the holidays.)

The tendency for companies I consult is to make a month-long sprint. I usually advocate for a lesser period because Sprint Recruiting is all about speed and agility. There are some instances when a month is feasible, but I'd encourage you to consider the benefits of shortening the time frame. Here is a couple:
1. Sprint Recruiting is about fast feedback – Faster responses from the client and quicker fill times.
2. This process is about continuous improvement – Shorter sprints=more opportunities to improve.

3. High-performance teams need the pressure to form – shorter sprints provide pressure and focus for the recruiting teams and the hiring managers. If the time frame is too long, both parties may procrastinate to the end of the sprint, defeating the purpose altogether. If you feel like your team starts by working at a leisurely pace at the start of a Sprint and then "cramming" at the end of the Sprint, shorter Sprints will force the team to work at a more even pace.
4. Small failures are better than large failures; shorter Sprints help. Which is better: "we spent four weeks building the wrong things" OR "we spent one week building the wrong things"? The iterative gains will be more significant if you shorten the sprint.
5. When a team is new or new to Sprint Recruiting, shorter Sprints help the team learn its capacity (also known as velocity) faster. It will help you to estimate coverage and define success more accurately as you progress through the year.

Again, the length of time for a sprint is unique to every organization and team. My preference is to have failures happen in a smaller scope, which gives my team more time to modify the search strategy with our clients. If you are unsure about what length of time works best for you, test your ideas and measure the results. The time with the highest efficiency should be the period you choose.

Define The Sprint Workflow

Our team tested several workflows to find what works best. A successful implementation requires you to take as much of the decision making out of the process. It will allow you and your team to focus on meeting your clients' needs. To help you, I'd like to share the sprint workflow we adopted after several iterations. It has helped us turn specific tasks and touchpoints on auto-pilot and remain focused on filling our pointed positions each sprint. As with everything else in the book, you and your team will need to find what works best for you.

Day 1
- Meet with the client to complete a retrospective meeting and allocate points for the new sprint.
- Points are recorded on your report or tracking tool.
- Recruiters use this information to time-block the next two days of the sprint based on analysis of where they are for each of the positions with points assigned.
- Emails are sent to the hiring managers who have roles given points alerting them they are "in the spotlight" and set expectations, get availability for interviews, and other needed admin work.

Day 3
- Recruiters do a quick check-in with the managers active in the sprint to give and receive an update.
- At this point, recruiters should be at or above 50% of their sourcing time block goal for the top 3 roles.
- If candidates have been sourced, this is a good time to do a fly-by with the manager to ensure the recruiter is on track with the sourcing strategy.
- Based on the managers' feedback, recruiters should take some time to time block the following two days.

Day 6
- Schedule a quick 15-minute check-in with active sprint job hiring managers to give updates, schedule interviewing blocks, or solicit feedback on interviews.

Day 10
- Recruiters should be 75% through the sourcing time block and approaching above 40% of points budgeted. (If you use 100 points budget, they should be at or above 40 points at this point.)
- Another checkpoint with hiring managers.
- It is a perfect time to provide a quick update to the Sprint Owner/Sprint Owner on the progress and obstacles experienced in the sprint thus far.
- Recruiters should plan and time-block the rest of the sprint.

Day 14
- Day 14 is the final push to close out the sprint and update any reporting tools for accuracy. It is vital to prepare for your retros with your clients and evaluate the sprint's progress as a leader.

- Recruiters should also prepare for the upcoming sprint and get a jumpstart on time-blocking.

One success tip I would share is to book calendar appointments for each of these. Some team members have an hour blocked off on the days listed above to complete the needed tasks to keep the sprint moving towards success. The commitment to these critical tasks on the assigned days will improve your sprint efficiency, so be sure to discuss with your team what is the best method.

Have a Sprint Zero

Before you dive headlong into sprint recruiting with your client, it's a good idea to have a sprint 0. In this sprint, you and your team can assign points to requisitions you feel are most important to the client and begin testing the framework and reporting before going live. Our first two sprints were without client involvement during our beta versions of Sprint Recruiting. It allowed us to test several aspects of sprint recruiting before going full-on with the client and creating more issues than we needed to manage.

Once you've assigned your fake points to the roles, begin conducting your daily stand-ups with the team, focusing on the roles assigned points. Sprint 0 is a great way to help your team get used to only discussing updates and obstacles for the sprint roles. Our team had a hard time staying on track initially, but as we began holding each other accountable, our meetings became more effective. It helped us grow closer as a team and identify any mindset shifts we needed to address before going live with our client.

It is also the perfect time to test your reporting. You may begin your reporting with 15 columns of information but find during Sprint 0, some of the data is not worth tracking. The ability to discover this information before involving clients will save you a lot of time and headache when you go live. There is nothing worse than creating more work for yourself while also confusing your client.

The length of Sprint 0 is entirely up to you. I mentioned our team used two sprints for a beta, primarily because we were creating the sprint methodology from scratch. You may find working in one test sprint gives you all the time you need to go live with your client. Only you and your team will be able to define the proper amount of time.

Set up your reporting

Unfortunately, most applicant tracking systems are ill-equipped to run sprint recruiting. For our sprints, I do a data dump every other Monday into a Google Sheet for the recruiters to update. The sheet contains the information we found most valuable. Remember, when you decide what information to include, be sure to keep your client at the center of the conversation. Your working document will be used to track key performance indicators for the sprint and should also include other common report requests in your organization.

Your team should agree to the frequency reporting should be updated. For most of our team, the sheet is used as a dashboard to focus on a sprint's roles. It's become an addiction to know where we are as a team each day before our standup. As a result, our team updates the main document daily to satisfy our need to evaluate progress and keep our clients updated as well. If you develop your reporting with the client's needs at the center, it will save you the time spent on miscellaneous report requests.

If you would like to download a free template, go to https://sprintrecruiting.com/resources/. I also offer more complex reporting services; if the simple template doesn't work for you, use the Contact Me page to schedule some time.

When I cover the sprint ideology with some colleagues, they doubt the value working on a timeline can provide. I hear how their recruiting process takes longer, so the sprint wouldn't work or how the client wouldn't adapt to estimating what positions should be filled during a defined timeframe.

I like to use Sabre as an example of how sprints can help create and manage efficiencies.

Sabre has created what they call Sprint Week- a five-day process for answering critical business questions through design, prototyping, and testing ideas with customers. It used the sprint within enterprise-level project processes, the Software Development Life Cycle (SDLC), and individual project teams and departments. The goal was to take six teams of 32 employees to create better solutions in a fraction of the time typically spent. These Sprint teams worked together throughout the week to build an informed prototype for customer testing on Friday.

The teams were given a loose framework to work from to accomplish their goal. On Monday, they were to map out a potential solution. Day 2 was dedicated to sketching out the road map so that on day 3, the team could come together to decide the proper course of actions needed to create a prototype. There are no pitch decks or exhaustive agendas for the meetings. Everything was stripped down to the bare essentials to facilitate the healthy dialogue needed to vet a solution properly.

Once decided, the team spent day 4 on their prototype to present at the end of the week to the end-user for feedback. The prototype could have been as simple as a cardboard box showing what a product could look like or a mock application indicating how they propose to streamline a complicated process. Regardless of the method, the prototype's goal was to solicit feedback from the client before moving into the next sprint. The process was fast and iterative, but all with the client as the center of every decision.

At the end of the sprint, the team would review its process to identify what worked to scale the activity, process, or behavior in the next sprint. They also identified obstacles and possible solutions to enable even more efficiency in the following sprints.

Sprint Week proved successful for the firm. The Sabre website states that as more teams are exposed to the Sprint Method's power, the firm expects to form a rapid-iteration framework that will define its business's future.

The efficiencies produced through each iterative sprint will allow you and your team to move quicker and with fewer obstacles. We'll discuss some of the critical metrics of Sprint Recruiting later in the book and how you will be able to observe how your team will respond quickly to the needs of your client sprint over sprint. The shorter time frame allows for quicker testing of improvement ideas in a safe environment. If you decide to test something and it fails, you've only lost two weeks to discover an idea that doesn't work.

The sprint will also ensure your team will quickly respond to the rapid changes in your business and the industry. The sprint's speed will require an adjustment, but the benefits far outweigh the struggles you and your team will endure adjusting to the new normal of sprinting.

Key Points to Remember for Sprints

1. You define the length of time but hold to it.
2. The Sprint allows you to focus your efforts on moving the needle on the critical roles of a set time frame.
3. The sprint will help you and your team maximize efficiencies by creating capacity within the team to do more in a shorter amount of time.
4. Define a workflow for the team to follow to create a cadence of work, avoiding the chaos of traditional recruiting.

Feedback drives Progress

I have been fascinated with Netflix since 2008. Over the last several years, I've been curious about how the company continues to raise the bar. One of the product deliverables I am obsessed with as a client is the platform's ability to know what I might want to watch next.

Think back to a time before Netflix. Maybe you just finished a series about the English dynasty that led to Queen Elizabeth's crowning. You might find yourself a little depressed that the series came to an end but decided to find something equally as appealing. Before Netflix, clients would stand in the isles of a movie store, aimlessly looking at titles to find something of interest. Some might engage an employee to get recommendations, but the value of that recommendation was mostly dependent on a mutual love for royal drama series. The chances you would walk out of the store with a series you would enjoy was roughly 50/50.

Now, let's think about how Netflix approaches this problem. The platform recognizes that you completed a three-season series on the subject in a recent binge-watching weekend. Rather than hopelessly scouring the list of titles in the Netflix library, the platform suggests five new series similar to the one you just completed.

You didn't have to ask anyone for help or wonder how in the world you'd replace the characters you fell in love with. Netflix knows what would be the best recommendation for you. For me, it saves me time and the headache of trying to determine which series I should binge next. It's right there on the screen, and all I have to do is play.

The amount of data Netflix gathers from its users is one of the key components in its success and profitability. It has evolved from its first attempt to cater content based on general themes to ranking your homepage with recommendations by genre, topic, time period, and even what's trending with other users similar to you. Each piece of data is gathered in real-time to enhance your experience and create committed customers. If Netflix did not collect and act on client feedback quickly, it would have suffered the same fate as chain movie stores.

The feedback loop in the recruiting process is equally as important. It must be as quick and efficient as possible to ensure the sprint is successful. When you place feedback requirements and deadlines, you will begin to notice slight efficiencies early on. It's when both the recruiter and the hiring manager solidify their partnership and commitment to achieving success in the sprint that the fun starts.

1. Managers become trained to know to see more candidates, they have to provide feedback to open slots in the WIP limit.
2. Recruiters become addicted to moving candidates through the process to close positions and collect points, creating innovative ways to hold managers to the deadline.
3. Candidates benefit the most by enjoying a quicker hiring process or by receiving the necessary feedback to grow in their career in a timelier manner.

During my training in Agile, one of the most powerful tools in the Agile process is the feedback loop. Similarly, sprint recruiting is an iterative, incremental, and collaborative approach to talent acquisition. The goal is to satisfy hiring managers through early and continuous delivery of candidates. Frequent feedback keeps the acquisition team focused on the client's top priorities and helps ensure they deliver high-value and qualified candidates. Equally important, feedback loops allow the team to accommodate change later in the development process, particularly as new or refined requirements emerge.

That's why we created built-in checkpoints to facilitate feedback and collaboration. The first step is the daily standup, allowing members of the recruiting team to share status updates and identify obstacles. The quick sprint review meetings with the hiring manager can present incremental updates with the client and gather feedback on the candidates presented. Lastly, the sprint retrospective allows the recruiting and executive team to look back at what went well and what could be done better in future sprints.

Sprint recruiting is designed to cultivate and enforce a culture of constant and candid feedback. The culture of sprint recruiting has helped our team achieve goals we did not think were attainable. This chapter on feedback will be relatively short, but please do not discount this principle. It will either make or break your success in implementing the sprint recruiting methodology in your organization. We will explore the following topics together over the next few pages:
1. Setting a deadline for feedback
2. The importance of honesty in your feedback culture
3. Mindsets to avoid regarding feedback
4. A look at how one organization leveraged feedback to transform their delivery to market

Setting a deadline for feedback.

In the book, I mentioned how I decided to export candidate data to determine how long it took a candidate to make it through our process. I had to check my math a couple of times because I honestly could not believe the average length of time a candidate could spend in our process was 67 days. We are not Google or Facebook, so it wasn't like candidates were beating down our doors to join the firm. We didn't have the notoriety for demanding that level of patience from candidates looking for a change in their career. More importantly, it was absurd to require a passive candidate to endure a 67-day journey to join the firm.

One afternoon before sprint recruiting was a fully vetted methodology, I sat at my desk, staring at a bar chart showing our candidate journey. I'm a data nerd and love digging in to see what story data is telling. I will often play around with the numbers to vet my hypothesis because the answer to my question is a bit elusive. Not this time. I was looking at a bar chart that showed two considerable bottlenecks in the process. I'm not talking about two bars slightly above the rest. I'm describing two glaring bars that were 15+ points above the others—the two stages when candidates became trapped involved getting feedback from managers. The first was awaiting feedback from the manager on the candidate's resume and recruiter write up. The second was after the hiring manager had interviewed them.

We aren't talking about waiting a couple of days for feedback. The average length of time for both stages was over 15 days. TWO WEEKS! It took an average of two weeks to get feedback from our managers on potentially qualified candidates who had been interviewed by someone at the company. It was mind-blowing and depressing to see the statistics.

Previous to charting this information, I spent a lot of my time on the phone with hiring managers who seemed to enjoy calling me to complain about their open roles not being filled quickly enough by recruiters. Of course, my job is to ensure all of my clients are happy, but about 80% of the time, the obstacle to filling the position is not the shortage of talent presented but the length of time it takes for managers to provide feedback on the candidate.

Some managers would interview great candidates and get a case of FOMO or fear of missing out on another "great" candidate who was out there somewhere. They would want to interview ten or fifteen candidates only to finally decide to pick one of the first five interviewed. Of course, by the time they decided, the qualified candidate had accepted another role or lost interest in our firm. We would then start the process repeatedly and recreate the chaos while our candidate experience and the brand suffered in the market.

When we began testing sprint recruiting, the feedback was not one of the principles. We assumed as we became more efficient, we would have more time to track down the feedback on the roles. While the efficiencies of sprint recruiting did allow us to accomplish this, we were still only reducing the candidate journey by a few days. We wanted to see a more significant reduction, so we began focusing on the principle *Feedback Drives Progress*.

Think of sprint recruiting as a vehicle, and feedback is the gas to keep it moving. It should happen often and should have a deadline to maximize efficiency. We determined the feedback needed to be a principle to keep the process moving and establish mutual accountability.

We tried various deadlines while building out the sprint recruiting methodology. Our first iteration required feedback in 24 hours, which we realized early on was a bit unrealistic. Things happen on both sides that can prevent someone from being available to give the necessary feedback. Additionally, we desired quality feedback, not just feedback for the sake of feedback. We wanted to provide our clients with enough time to review the information and make an informed decision. If not, we would find ourselves in the same feedback loop just more often.

Our team decided on 48 hours because it gave enough time to evaluate the candidate's qualifications and gave the recruiters enough time to work on other positions in the sprint. The 24-hour limit caused recruiters to stop too often to receive feedback and adjust their strategy. This cut into the focus time to source candidates for the other priority roles. If the limit were any longer, we would have too much dead time, and we could lose out on good candidates. Once a manager conducts an interview, they have 48 hours to provide feedback to the recruiter. WIP limits helped create stopgaps to prevent managers from requesting 15 or more candidates to interview. It trained the managers to give feedback to receive more candidates.

Let's look at the feedback stages of sprint recruiting and discuss how to make minor improvements to create maximum efficiencies in your progress.

The first stage is what I call a "fly-by" list of candidates to ensure I'm on the right track. It's an excellent way to zero in on the right candidate profile and not spend time trying to develop a candidate the manager feels is not a fit. I can read a job description, but all of us know there are things not listed in a job description critical to a candidate's success in a role.

When a job enters sprint for the first time, it's paramount to work on this fly-by list of candidates on Day 1 or 2 to maximize your time. This is why it's vital to time block those first two days to source for your critical roles. They detail the expectation of quick feedback during the first two days to ensure both the manager and the recruiter are looking for the same level of a candidate. The fly-by list of candidates is an efficient way to accomplish this.

There is a difference between the generic feedback loop involved in traditional recruiting versus the sprint recruiting method.

Traditional Recruiting	**Sprint Recruiting**
Each activity like the search strategy design, development, testing (fly-by) is considered as an individual phase.	All the activities are done in a smaller time cycle. The constraint of the sprint paired with the points assigned for priority emphasizes the mandate to get feedback on presented candidates often and quickly.
The customer typically reviews candidates at the end of the initial search. Any changes to the needs of the manager or the search strategy involve significant rework. This increases the hidden costs of the search: recruiter time, loss of productivity, and loss of efficiency.	If the feedback is obtained within days, it may be very easy for the team to make quick changes and increase the potential for more qualified candidates quicker.
Those roles most critical to the firm may be lost in the shuffle in traditional recruiting. Roles with hiring managers who procrastinate	The business and the recruiter are focused on the highest priority roles so there is mutual accountability and partnership

in the feedback process may cost the recruiter a lot of time and recruiters tend to move to where the fire is.	in the feedback process.

Once the recruiter has received the necessary feedback from the manager on their fly-by candidates, they can use their sourcing time block to focus on the role. For our team, the WIP limit of the second swim lane (Submitted for Hiring Manager Review) is 5, so the recruiter's goal is to take the feedback from the fly-by and retool to find a max of 5 qualified candidates.

Candidates identified and screened by the recruiter are then sent to the hiring manager to review. If we find our max of five qualified candidates to submit, we've hit our WIP limit, so we move on to the next role in priority until feedback is received. This stage is where recruiters struggled a bit during our initial launch of sprint recruiting. The initial inclination was to continue to source and interview candidates beyond the five without receiving feedback from the manager. It was a mindset shift for recruiters to move on to the next role guilt-free.

The managers have 48 hours to review the candidates and provide feedback. We found the managers were motivated by the WIP limits. When a manager who had five candidates in their cue asked for more, we reminded them that we needed feedback on which candidates they were interested in moving to the next stage before we sent more. We used their FOMO in our favor to speed up the process and reduce the time the job was open.

We also evolved our process to include notating a status in our report to show when we had reached our WIP limit for a role. It proved incredibly helpful for us to be able to move through our dashboards every morning quickly. The status reminded us to check in with managers to get feedback on the candidates presented and not spend any more time sourcing for that role. It also helped our sprint owners know which positions were being held up by the manager versus the recruiter. The level of mutual accountability and transparency created a level of efficiency we were not expecting. Rather than spending time on the phone, giving an update, or trying to defend our efforts, everyone could see the lack of feedback created an obstacle. Usually, when the sprint owners would identify roles at their WIP limits, they would reach out to the hiring manager with a friendly prompt to keep the process going. This was when we realized we were on to something.

Now that you have feedback from the manager on who they want to move to the interview stage, there is another feedback moment. Recruiters need to work with the manager to determine if the candidates to be interviewed are qualified enough to hire or if we need to source a couple more as a reserve. It accounts for the third feedback stop in the process. We discovered that as managers became used to the sprint recruiting process, the need to interview ten thousand candidates diminished. They realized their roles were given points, which meant senior management evaluated how quickly we moved as a team to hire the most qualified candidate.

The transparency of our process and reporting reframed their analysis of candidates in most cases. Sure, we still had the managers who felt the need to interview droves of candidates, but the percentage of managers who fell into that category diminished. We noticed the increase in communication points worked in conjunction with the feedback requirements to enable us to move quicker on candidates than before.
Managers became accustomed to how quickly we could get their roles filled, which only increased their tendency to respond quickly. I think the requirements we placed on ourselves also helped foster an efficient feedback loop. Everyone involved had committed to and performed to the 48-hour deadline.

The recruiters initially liked the idea of setting a deadline for managers but didn't appreciate the commitment we had to make to enforce it. If you have ten critical roles in your sprint, stopping your schedule to receive the necessary feedback on your progress can appear to be a drain on your time. I had to work with them to overcome this mental block. We limited the check-in meetings with managers to either an email or a 15-minute call. We did not want to sacrifice too much sourcing and screening time while obtaining the necessary feedback.

The recruiters eventually began to trust the process. There was one challenging role a team member was attempting to achieve her WIP limit. She shared with me in a one on one how much she dreaded the check-in call with the manager the following day. She had already submitted three qualified candidates but found it a struggle to get two more. Her hiring manager was a stickler for rules, so she felt he would be disappointed and withhold feedback on the three until she met her WIP. To her surprise, the manager told her to stop looking because he loved the three already submitted. Without the feedback rule, the recruiter would have lost valuable time she could have dedicated to other roles in the sprint. That is the value of the feedback principle.

Determining your deadline will be relatively easy compared to enforcing the deadline. We discussed the 48-hour deadline with our clients during their sprint training. When we communicated the feedback principle with our clients, heads nodded, and everyone agreed this was doable. Sprint 1 always proved how hard it was for our clients and the recruiting team to honor the deadline.

Our team has two statuses in our report used to track sprint progress. The first is the obvious "Hiring Manager Interviewing." I noticed how recruiters became obsessed with moving jobs to and collecting points that naturally motivated them to ask for managers' feedback. Early adopters on our team would use reminders in their calendar, Candidate Relationship System (CRM), or note-taking routine to ensure they managed the 48-hour window.

Initially, some of our more challenging managers would become agitated by frequent feedback requests on candidates presented. (Ironic, huh?) However, over time, we conditioned most of our hiring teams to provide feedback on candidates before the 48-hour time limit, allowing us to move quicker on the right candidates. The ability to track how many critical roles we filled in a sprint fostered a motivation point for our managers to retrain themselves regarding the length of time taken to provide candidate feedback.

The second status we added later in our implementation process was "WIP Limit." We realized the Hiring Manager Interviewing status did not tell us when we had reached the maximum number of candidates in that swim lane. It was problematic for recruiters who would review their dashboard daily to plan their day. The ambiguous status caused recruiters to stop and check how many candidates were in the process. Although this didn't take that much time, it was still an inefficiency we corrected when we implemented this status.

The WIP Limit status also allowed our Sprint Owner to see their call to action quickly. If a requisition stayed in this status for more than two days, the more engaged sprint owners would take the responsibility of contacting the hiring manager to add some "motivation." It allowed our team to get out of policing the process and spend more time sourcing candidates. It also created another accountability point with our clients.

I am reminded of one particular situation when the WIP Limit status proved impactful. I had one client who seemed to enjoy making our team a whipping post for all things wrong with their department. It was the typical complaints we all hear: "We don't see enough candidates," "You don't move quick enough," etc. When the sprint owner scheduled a meeting to review their list of complaints, I provided them the link to our tracking report to start the conversation.

Their group had roughly 25 positions open, with 8 of them assigned points. Out of the 8 positions, 5 of them were at the WIP limit of 5 candidates. I had already met with recruiters before this meeting to ask where we were in the feedback process. All five managers had been at their WIP limit for at least four days. It was all I needed to know going into the meeting.

The meeting lasted roughly fifteen minutes. I began the meeting by reminding the sprint owner of the four sprint recruiting principles before going into the report. Once I highlighted the principle that feedback was to be given within 48 hours, the sprint owner cut me off.

"I think I know where you are going with this. How long has it been since you requested feedback on the requisitions at their WIP limit?"
Me: "At least four days."

"Ok, let me rattle some cages. Seems like the story I am getting from the department is not entirely accurate. Thank you for the clarification."

That was the last time I had to have that conversation with the department. Establishing the deadline and holding our clients accountable to it eliminated the back and forth accusations of traditional recruiting and increased our ability to move quicker on qualified candidates.

Candidate Feedback

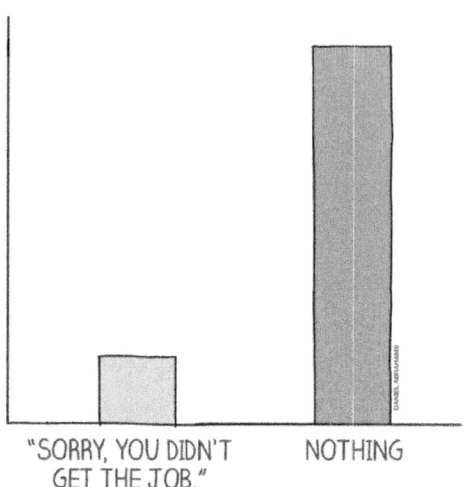

The deadline is not only applicable to your hiring managers. Recruiters must provide interview feedback to candidates within the 48-hour window as well. The graphic from Daniel Abrahams is a deafening blow to the recruiting industry. If you think about the amount of time you spend developing candidates and selling them on your brand, we are ethically bound to provide the feedback they deserve.

We found that traditional recruiting did not allow us to spend the necessary time with those declined due to either not receiving the feedback promptly or our lack of commitment to closing the loop. Unfortunately, we were not the only recruiting team missing the mark in this part of the process. According to Paul Slezak's article, there are two main why this happens:

- **Priorities:** If a candidate is no longer considered for a job, calling them back is not as important to a

recruiter, hiring manager, or business owner as meeting their other deadlines.
- **Procrastination:** Being the bearer of bad news is not a pleasant task for anyone, and a hiring manager or recruiter may just be putting it off until they have a spare moment. Unfortunately, that moment often never comes.

In a candidate-driven market, this can cause severe damage to your employer brand. When you do not provide negative feedback, your brand suffers as candidates begin sharing your lack of response within their network.

We had a significant push to hire ten critical, highly technical, and in-demand roles in 45 days to meet a recent audit requirement. This period was before we implemented sprint recruiting, so we were in the chaos of sourcing and screening as many candidates as we could find. At one point, we had 15 candidates in the interview process, but no one kept track of this type of information. The managers were suffering from both FOMO and over-analysis paralysis. Candidates were dropping out of the process, and we soon discovered the consequences of not providing feedback on time.

I jumped in to help source and screen since this was a Level 1 emergency. I had cold-called five candidates one day only to have three of them inform me they were not interested. When I diplomatically pressed them for a reason, they told me we had a bad reputation of interviewing people and never following up. It was for that reason the candidates did not want to invest the time in learning more about the opportunity. As a leader, this was a gut punch for two reasons. First, we were losing the opportunity to attract candidates because of a branding issue. The second was because it was something we had 100% control over.

Ironically, a declined candidate might tell a friend about their positive experience if handled appropriately. On the other hand, a disgruntled candidate will tell at least ten friends how appalled they were with their experience. And there's no stopping the damage they could bring to your (and your company's) reputation when they begin their social media campaign. It is imperative to implement more quality checks and protocols around the candidate experience – especially when it comes to candidate rejection.

Mindset to avoid

I shared how many managers were disgruntled when we began requiring quick feedback. The team's natural inclination was to wait until the biweekly client call to solicit feedback as a way to avoid this. It is a common mindset you will have to change to become successful in sprint recruiting.

While it's always a good idea to please your client, I'd argue that waiting until even the end of a sprint is too long to solicit feedback. The recruiting process is similar to the butterfly effect, where, especially early in the process, minor changes can result in large differences downstream. This is particularly true for job searches with unclear or changing requirements. Without the opportunity to discuss and validate managers' needs early and often, recruiters will inevitably make assumptions that unchecked, could steer the search, of course. The definition of a qualified candidate will become increasingly harder to unravel as the sprint progresses.

One of my favorite quotes about feedback in the Agile process is from Henrik Kniberg and Mattias Skarin. In their book *Kanban and Scrum: Making the Most of Both,* the authors provide this great advice:
Generally speaking, you want as short a feedback loop as possible so that you can adapt your process quickly.

To enable short feedback loops both during and after sprints, recruiting teams can leverage points as the common language that creates mutual understanding between the hiring team and the recruiting function. The point system helps set the definition of success and facilitates constant communication and collaboration to ensure that the right roles are being focused on. Recruiters can use the value of the job (points) to create a call to action for both teams to commit to frequent feedback to keep the process moving. Regular feedback is vital for recruiting teams to understand whether they are going in the direction as expected and defined by the client.

When you or your team feel the need to back off the feedback deadline, I will encourage you to press even harder. The breakthrough occurs when you begin seeing positive trends in the number of points you can obtain during a sprint. More time will be spent sourcing the right candidates, based on timely feedback from the managers, which will translate to a more engaged recruiting team and much happier clients.

Radical Candor Feedback

I had the opportunity to work with some startups over my career as a consultant. There's something addictive about the culture of deadlines and the need to prove themselves to the market. There's an inherent drive with most successful startups that are driven by the need for quick results. Successful companies have learned that quick feedback is not the only necessity for success but also most powerful when it's brutally honest.

This tends to be an issue for most larger corporations trained to death by an HR culture of fear in honest communication. I've worked with managers who spent more time trying to sugar coat how to communicate performance issues with team members than they did communicate with the team. Radical feedback is not insensitive, but it also isn't known for dancing around the subject.

Kim Scott's book entitled "Radical Candor" outlines the process to create this culture. To receive radically candid criticism from an unwilling team, Scott suggests that you spend a couple of weeks doing the following:
1. Don't let people off the hook when they refuse to give feedback. Keep asking, and then use silence to get them to say something.
2. Reward them handsomely for their criticism. Thank them, praise them, most notably: take action to fix their criticism if you can.

3. Scott argues that you should be soliciting guidance every day, in one-to-two minute conversations between engagements, not in scheduled meetings on your calendar. (To drive this point home, Scott tells the story of Sheryl Sandberg actively chasing a banker for feedback — during Facebook's IPO process! Sandberg was relentless in her desire for improvement).

The concept of Radical Candor is vital for the sprint process, especially during the biweekly meetings with your team and the client. We began our biweekly meetings with our clients during our pilot by outlining the ground rules for our version of Radical Candor. We encouraged everyone to share their feedback openly but raw, real, and respectful. One of the major rules was for the feedback to be brutally honest and helpful in its delivery.

This was a major culture shift for many of our clients, who tended to share direct feedback about recruiting only with my boss or me. To change this mindset, I worked with those I had control over to set the tone. I challenged the team to be open and honest during our client meetings about our obstacles. My commitment to my team was that I would provide the cover fire they needed when they brought to the meeting credible obstacles. Fortunately or unfortunately, I can be a bit of a jerk when I need to, so it's not an issue for me to push back when required, especially intense situations.

The first couple of feedback sessions made slightly more progress than the other, but nothing out of the polite ordinary. One particular sprint's performance was impacted by the lack of involvement from some key members of leadership within a division. They had indicated these roles were critical yet pushed interviews out two weeks, inhibiting our ability to meet the definition of success they had set just a week before. The recruiters were more than reluctant to bring this up as an obstacle for fear the clients would retaliate during the call. Well, I thought this would be an excellent time for us to test the waters of our new feedback style.

The recruiter most impacted identified the lengthy interview process as an obstacle to the process on the call. Almost on cue, one of the executives began to give a "get over it speech" when I politely intervened.

> *Me: "Hey, we agreed that critical roles would require all of us to move schedules around to keep active candidates engaged in the process. Correct?"*
>
> *Executive: Yes but....*
>
> *Me: There isn't an excuse right? Did we agree to open feedback right?*
> *Executive: We did.*
>
> *Me: Ok, great. So now that we know you all created the barrier to success, how can we work together to avoid this in sprints in the future? This isn't an attack or anything, we just have to find a way to get around scenarios like this. It creates a lack of productivity for us and you lose out on great candidates. Thoughts?*

This opened a dialogue with our client that produced additional commitment from that department to realign schedules to value interviewing over various meetings. It was not a contentious conversation in tone, but it was confrontational in context. The rules we had set early on allowed us to identify an obstacle in the process and discuss solutions to avoid similar situations in the future in a constructive way.

While this is a short chapter, I would encourage you to vet this principle with your recruiting team and managers thoroughly. The initial pains will soon be replaced with efficiencies, accountability, and balance as you sprint on toward happy candidates and engaged managers.

By the way, if you haven't read Kim Scott's book on Radical Candor, let me plug it. It'll help you in the feedback process with your team members, clients, and even candidates who do not get the job. Definitely check it out.

The Mindset Shift

Before getting into the nuts and bolts of creating a successful sprint, it's essential to address one of the primary obstacles you and your team will face during this time: your mindset. The amount of change you will be implementing can become overwhelming for all involved. One of the most helpful tips for managing through this is from the Heath Brothers' Book *Switch*.

According to the authors:
> In times of change, you need what my brother and I call a bright-spots focus. That is, you need to look for the early glimmers that something is going right. And when you find a bright spot, your mission is to study it and clone it.

The way to help overcome the sense of pending failure is to begin focusing on these bright spots. They may be small movements toward success that would typically get overlooked or ignored in light of the cluster of mistakes or obstacles you may encounter. It's through the celebration of the small wins that will help get your team and clients focused on the positive movements during the sprint and look for ways to scale.

It's common for an anxious mind to block logic and reason. It is no surprise that one of the most pressing obstacles in our transition to sprint recruiting was the mindset shift is required. I am sure the principles seem pretty easy and straightforward as you read through the book, but putting them into practice will be more of a struggle than you anticipate.

I've found it helpful to force myself to think like an entrepreneur. If you compare the mindset of an employee of a large corporation to that of an entrepreneur, you'll see a stark difference in how they approach change. Entrepreneurs tend to run toward high risk and high reward scenarios compared to corporate employees' more conservative mindset. Many of us have worked so long in the corporate world, we've lost that innovative flare and ability to change

our mindsets quickly. According to Entrepreneur.com, there are some easy steps to think less like a corporate clog and more like innovative entrepreneurs:
1. Set goals and make daily progress on them
2. Learn to be comfortable with being uncomfortable
3. Be ok with healthy risks
4. Spend time with other entrepreneurs

The first step on your journey to a more entrepreneurial mindset is built into the sprint methodology. The obstacle most face with any change is the idea of doing a 180-degree change in 24 hours. Making small, incremental changes can allow your brain to adjust to the new routines and habits.

The idea of running toward the uncomfortable is instinctively counterintuitive. Our brains are wired to fight or fly when we feel threatened, so it's not uncommon to feel as though you have to force yourself to push through certain situations. One of my friends had a quote from his military days, "Embrace the suck." He shared how this thought process got him through training when his body told him to quit. In most situations, when things get a little uncomfortable, your brain must be rewired to push through the pain and find the breakthrough.

Once you learn to embrace the suck, you'll become more comfortable with healthy risks. Think of all of the fairytale startup stories with entrepreneurs taking a risk that seemed wildly unwise, only to rake in cash. It doesn't always happen that way but taking small risks over time helps you become less averse to risk and gives you a baseline to understand when it is wise to take a leap of faith.

I can understand the importance of spending time with other entrepreneurs. While I don't desire a cornucopia of yes-men, I also do not need negative and fixed-minded people in my life. I will seek out those who will keep it real with me while also helping me vet out innovative ideas. Find a group to help support you through the implementation who are wise, honest, candid, and innovative. They will become your lifeline on the days you want to throw in the towel.

There are three types of changes you will experience based on our journey.

Leading the transformation from Fixed to a Growth Mindset

Stanford University psychologist Carol Dweck was curious why some people in life thrive while others flounder. As she studied the motivation for success and achievement for over four decades, she discovered a significant distinction between a fixed mindset and a growth mindset.

Those who operate in a fixed mindset tend to believe they are either born with talent, or they're not. It is a binary view of nature versus nurture approach to success. Typically, they will view intelligence as a fixed trait and believe inborn talent determines success. Individuals with a fixed mindset seek to validate themselves and will oppose data contrary to their core beliefs.

Because they believe their intelligence and abilities are what they are, they invest their energy in looking smart instead of learning and developing. They will attempt new hobbies or learn new behaviors, but their tolerance for failure is much lower. As a result, they tend to avoid challenges for fear of being judged as a failure if they cannot excel in a short timeframe. They often exhibit primal responses to constructive feedback because of their inability to accept failure.

Abraham Maslow called it "aborted self-actualization." He wrote in The Farther Reaches of Human nature:

If you deliberately plan to be less than you are capable of being, then I warn you that you'll be deeply unhappy for the rest of your life. You will be evading your own capacities, your own possibilities.

The opposing mindset is called the growth mindset. Those with this mindset believe they can develop any ability through dedication and hard work. This core belief drives them to be continuous learners and has a natural curiosity about the world. They tend to embrace challenges and persevere when setbacks invariably arise during the learning process. This group will view effort as an essential ingredient on the path to mastery. When they view team members or others succeeding on their path to mastery, they use it as inspiration, often seeking advice from such individuals as a way to continue their growth journey.

Dweck offers a self-test in her Mindset book. Take a moment to read each of the following statements and decide whether you mostly agree or disagree:
1. Your intelligence is something fundamental about you that you can't change very much.
2. You can learn new things, but you can't change how intelligent you are.
3. No matter how much intelligence you have, you can always change it quite a bit.
4. You can always substantially change how intelligent you are.

Questions 1 and 2 reflect a fixed-mindset—questions 3 and 4 point to a growth mindset.

Here's an example from PositivePsychology.com on the difference between the fixed and growth mindset:

Running late and missing the bus or carpool.
You've certainly been here before: your alarm doesn't go off (or maybe you hit snooze a few too many times), and you oversleep. You jump out of bed and race into your clothes, skipping any part of your morning ritual that isn't completely necessary before racing outside to catch the bus. As you run to the street, you see the bus pulling away, and you know you're going to be late.

For someone with a fixed mindset, this scenario might ruin their whole day. They may feel angry with themselves or look for someone or something else to blame.

On the other hand, someone with a growth mindset is more likely to think about the root cause of the mess they're in and consider how to avoid it next time. They may conclude that they need to go to bed earlier tonight or set their alarm a little bit louder. The point is, the person with a growth mindset will think about ways to fix the problem because they believe it is fixable.

Understanding these mindsets will be vital as you facilitate the change in your organization to Sprint Recruiting. You may have to shift your mindset before attempting to change that of your team or client. Perhaps you've already identified those on your team who have the fixed mindset and will need some extra coaching to embrace a new way of recruiting. According to Psychology Today, there are eight general approaches for developing the foundation for such a mindset:

1. **Create a new compelling belief**: a belief in yourself, in your skills and abilities, and your capacity for positive change.
2. **View failure in a different light**: see failure as an opportunity to learn from your experiences and apply what you have learned next time.
3. **Cultivate your self-awareness**: work on becoming more aware of your talents, strengths, and weaknesses; gather feedback from those who know you best and put it together for a comprehensive view of yourself.
4. **Be curious and commit to lifelong learning:** try to adopt the attitude of a child, looking at the world around you with awe and wonderment, ask questions, and truly listen to the answers.
5. Get friendly with challenges: know that if you mean to accomplish anything worthwhile, you will face many challenges on your journey; prepare yourself for meeting these challenges and for failing sometimes.
6. **Do what you love and love what you do:** it's much easier to succeed when you are passionate about what you're doing; whether you cultivate a love

for what you already do or focus on doing what you already love, developing passion is essential.
7. **Be tenacious:** it takes a lot of hard work to succeed, but it takes even more than working hard—you must be determined, weathering obstacles and getting back up after each time you fall.
8. **Inspire and be inspired by others:** it can be tempting to envy others when they succeed, especially if they go farther than you, but it will not help you to succeed; commit to being an inspiration to others and use the success of others to get inspiration as well.

I would recommend working with those on your team who have a fixed mindset well in advance of implementing sprint recruiting. Your team will need some extra time to prepare themselves for the journey, and it will help minimize potential obstacles early in the process.

If you're interested in hearing more about this theory, check out Carol Dweck's TED Talk on YouTube. She describes what prompted her to think about mindset, what the research on this subject has found, and the power of "yet."

There are three specific mindset journeys we experienced while developing Sprint Recruiting. The next couple of pages will walk you through the hard lessons we've already learned. I hope it saves you time and energy as you begin your transformation.

The Recruiting Leader Mindset Shift
"In God, we trust, everyone else must bring data."
William Edwards Demming

We adopted this quote for our journey. It was a way for me to filter out the typical emotional response to change and focus on what was true versus perceived. As your team and clients become accustomed to sprint recruiting, there will be typical growing pains and complaints to contend with. I found myself many times asking why in the hell I even thought to try something as crazy. It was those instances when I would go back to the data and analyze our progress. Most of the time, the data told a more positive story than what my emotions led me to believe.

The traditional recruiting model had me frazzled on most days. I would run from one fire to the next, unable to make progress on any team goals, much less have a method to track them. I think many leaders become addicted to the chaos and misconception that busy means productive. Focusing on more productive days versus busy was not hard for me to adopt, but it was hard for me to enforce. The fire drills are still a lure for me to slip into my old habits, but I've learned a little trick to keep me on course. When a request or situation arises requiring my attention, I will ask myself, "Is this busy or productive?" This simple pause and reflection allow me to categorize the request and adjust my response accordingly.

You will need to become a data-obsessed and data-informed leader to implement sprint recruiting successfully. Leading with data will begin to change the conversations you have with your team and clients towards more effective outcomes. Make a habit of starting your day reviewing the previous days to assess your team's progress. This habit will help you slowly retrain your mindset to focus on the data and align effort toward the terms of success your client-defined with their point allocation.

I found the data from our dashboards helped me do this. In addition to becoming more data-driven, you will have to remove the crutches from your team. Contrary to my rough exterior, I am a softy at heart, especially when it comes to my team. I want everyone to succeed and often go beyond a healthy level of support to help. You will need to find the delicate balance between supporter and enforcer, even more during sprint recruiting.

A step I found helpful during this evolution was to change the format of my one on ones. I currently have 27 members who I meet with a one on one biweekly. The form shared allows for data-driven, efficient meetings with my team.

There are times when it is necessary to divert from the agenda due to business or personal situations the team member may need to discuss, but for the most part, the agenda is locked. It has helped me avoid the co-dependent tendency I once had with my team.

Let me warn you. This behavior will not make a lot of friends once you implement it. One of the steps I took to help create a barrier was to create a rule in Gmail. When someone sent an invitation, they would receive a response template. It would first thank them for the meeting invite but inform them that I would only accept invites when an agenda was included in the invite or sent in a subsequent email. At first, it helped the number of useless meetings that sucked up the time I could be more productive. It was not well received by many senior leaders who found the email to be aloof and arrogant.

I no longer use this template because I began changing the behaviors of my colleagues. I am sure there are conversations like, "Don't invite him unless you have an agenda because he thinks his time is more valuable than yours....". Believe it or not, I sleep just fine at night because I am more productive when I own my calendar rather than allowing it to become a to-do list others have access to.

Another step in the Busy vs. Productive mindset change you will need to address is how this applies to your team. During our transformation, I learned how many times I allowed team members to engulf me in their hyped-up yet preventable dramas. When one of your team members calls with a situation, start by asking if the job to discuss has points assigned to it. If the answer is yes, continue the discussion. If not, ask yourself if the situation is that dire.

Over time, the team began to learn this trick and would send messages like, "Can I talk to you about my 30 pointer? I have an issue I need your insight on." Those requests would always get my attention. I had to retrain my mind not to feel guilty for only being concerned with roles assigned points. I would remind myself that the points are how my clients tell me what is important during the sprint. If they define it as a priority, I should too. It was a mindset shift for me because I have been trained to jump on every client crisis since I began my career. Realign your mindset to your client's priorities, and your day will become more harmonious and productive.

Perhaps the most challenging transition as a leader in this new recruiting methodology is releasing control. One of the core principles of Agile is the person closest to the client makes the decision. We adopted this idea in sprint recruiting, which forced me to change my leadership style. I would often feel the need to weigh in on every topic, which was exhausting at times. Of course, the team always could chart their course, but I found that they felt an instinctive need to bounce ideas off of me before executing.

As we implemented sprint recruiting throughout the organization, we began consolidating teams and removing barriers. The entire recruiting organization now reports to me directly, which can seem overwhelming if you viewed it on an organization chart. Fortunately, we have evolved over the last year, leveraging a culture of empowerment. There are countless decisions made daily requiring little to no involvement from me. The recruiters have the ability and responsibility to move quickly and efficiently towards the goals our clients define at the beginning of every sprint. I am sure recruiting leaders reading this might think this is a fairy tale scenario but let me encourage you to start with your mindset before retraining your team. Indulge me in a story to illustrate.

I was fortunate to manage a team of ten employees early in my career. I was young and power-hungry, so I involved myself in every decision to ensure my branch would succeed. Over time, my choices became less and less visionary, and I grew more tired as each day passed. I spoke with a mentor at the time who encouraged me to try a new tactic.

I was to buy a pack of the barrel of toy monkeys and place them on my desk. Those who might be too young to remember these toys were neon, plastic monkeys connected by their tails or arms. The game was quite simple. The first player takes their chosen monkey with great care and tries to use the monkey's arm to grab a second monkey from the pile. If the player successfully hooks a second monkey, they continue and try for a third monkey, then a fourth, and so on. It sounds boring, but it kept us entertained for hours growing up.

My mentor instructed me to take a toy monkey out of the barrel every time a team member brought a situation for me to weigh in. The goal was to be sure the toy monkey left with the employee and did not stay with me. Rather than giving an easy solution to the team member's questions, I helped them make the right decision by guiding them with questions or offering suggestions on how to resolve the matter themselves.

Before they left the office, they were to take the monkey with them. The idea was to remind me that I didn't have to solve every problem or find every possible solution myself. There was a weird sense of relief when the team member took the toy problem with them, and my focus would return to the tasks I needed to complete to be successful. The team members' goal was to return the monkey when they found the solution to the problem to discuss the decision process as a development opportunity.

I know this sounds like a corny exercise, but it did wonders for my personal and professional wellbeing. I also noticed the game empowered the team to find creative ways to solve client problems, so I would have never thought to achieve the same result. I didn't know it at the time, but I had just learned the Agile principle of "those closest to the clients making the decision."

During the first year, I learned how to shift from leading with control to leading with context. Leading with control is the antithesis of Sprint Recruiting and the root of a lot of manager fatigue. Team members working in this environment must run every major decision by their boss before proceeding. Folklore of leaders like Steve Jobs, who was known for being highly involved in every product decision, has created a more gilded disguise for micromanagement.

As a Sprint Recruiting leader, you must force yourself to strive to develop good decision-making behaviors throughout the team. I am not defining or suggesting complete hands-off management, though. Your new role is to teach your teams how to make decisions, set the context or a thought process for decisions, and be highly informed of what is happening.

Setting the context is more manageable than controlling everything. Rather than walking your team through each step of the process, you set the end goal or the business initiative the team needs to solve. The best way to learn how the context setting needs to improve is to explore a sample of the details. But unlike the micro-manager, the goal of knowing those details is not to change small decisions but to learn how to adjust context, so more decisions are made well.

As I began to evolve into our new methodology, I had to learn to force myself to ask team members, "How would you handle X situation considering our objectives?" This question opened the dialogue for us to have a meaningful conversation regarding possible solutions. It also gave me more of an understanding of how each member of the team approached problem-solving. I would use this feedback during the one on one times to delve deeper into the type of decision-making process that would make each member of the team more successful in our new model. Over time, the calls I would get was less of, "Help me solve this problem," and more "Let me walk you through what I'm thinking." It was a great transition for the team to take ownership of our evolution, and it freed a lot of my time to focus more on strategy and measuring success.

There are some minor exceptions to "context not control." The first would be early in the implementation process. It will be vital for you to set the course and guide your team through the mindset shift they will encounter. You will need to have many day-to-day decisions or problem-solving run through you until your team and client are more comfortable with the methodology. Even when Sprint Recruiting is implemented, there will be times when an urgent situation with little time to think about proper context and principles will require your attention.

Recap for Leaders:

1. Focus on the data
2. Avoid the busy and focus on the productive
3. Own your calendar, it cannot own you
4. Align your priorities and focus on how your client defines success and eliminates guilt.
5. Free yourself. Empower your team to make the decisions most impactful to your client.

The Recruiter Mindset Shift

Unraveling the unconscious mindset of recruiters in traditional recruiting can be daunting. Similar to my advice to leaders, recruiters are accustomed to equating busy with productive. This mindset is the first you will need to change to be successful. The time-blocking habit is one step to overcoming the bond recruiters have with chaos and busywork. I've yet to meet a successful recruiter who is not competitive. The idea of collecting points every sprint becomes a central motivator in the mindset transformation. To help with this shift, they'll need to start their day with the dashboard.

Every morning, have them sort their dashboard according to the number of points assigned to each role in descending order. This simple routine will retrain your mindset to focus more on what needs to be accomplished to meet your client's definition of success. Use the time blocking method to chart your day according to what tasks are most critical for moving the needle on your critical roles. Remember, it is important to schedule a time to follow up and administrative duties twice a day. Time blocks are, by design, for you to add the miscellaneous tasks that will inevitably attempt to disrupt your focus during the day. We have found this simple trick allows us to focus more on the sprint related tasks and less on the disruptive tendencies that will make you slip back into traditional recruiting.

It's also essential to create a team dynamic of accountability and candid feedback. When team members begin slipping into bad habits, the team should have the freedom to self-regulate. Our team started to self-manage more as I began releasing control and empowering them to govern how we achieved success. We are lucky that many on our team are incredibly open to feedback, which holds each other accountable. Work together and ask for help when you find yourself missing the mark with your sprint. Be open to the feedback you receive and allow it to help reform how you approach recruiting.

Recap for recruiters:

1. Time blocking is the key to success
2. Start your day with your dashboard
3. Encourage accountability among team members to help ensure success

The Hiring Manager Mindset Shift

If you thought changing your mindset would be the most challenging hurdle, let me prepare you for what's in store when you implement sprint with your client. Major retraining!

The Point System
Managers first struggled with the concept of allocating points to a select percentage of open positions. While they liked knowing those roles would receive particular focus, managers still wanted to be assured their jobs would be filled on time. Part of this mindset change will only happen when you begin to experience success in sprint recruiting. It usually takes the second or third sprint for your partners to grasp that you commit to filling the critical roles ahead of those deemed non-critical.

This mindset obstacle is another reason we instituted the concept of assigning "extra credit" points to roles filled during the sprint deemed non-critical. Charting this information helped us slowly ease the manager's minds that we would not abandon any position without points. It also enabled us to quantify how often these roles prevented us from achieving our goal, as outlined in previous chapters.

We had another mindset obstacle with managers early on when assigning points. If they had ten open roles and 100 points, their idea was to give every role ten points. There was some pushback when we placed a limit on the number of roles and spread of points. You will have to reinforce the improved focus and ability sprint recruiting gives you to close the critical roles. Again, this mindset will slowly fade as you begin proving how successful you can close these roles during the sprint.

The Sprint
The concept of using a sprint is equally as challenging for your hiring partners. I cannot count how many times I would have to remind our clients that we were assigning priority for only the next two weeks. Breaking the mindset that everything is a priority is a hard one to overcome. Many hiring partners have become so accustomed to the frantic need to fill every open position that the addiction becomes deeply rooted.

Iteration is the key to the sprint recruiting approach. Instead of tackling a colossal requisition workload all at once, it's broken down into individual tasks, which are then grouped into your two-week "sprints." You will need to guide your hiring partners on how to redefine the scope. Unfortunately, there is no silver bullet to adjust this mindset except repetition in the process. Your clients will slowly become used to a more defined scope as you enter your third sprint.

I have to confess there were several times when I doubted the effectiveness of this new methodology. Although I felt it showed some initial signs of success, I always had a sneaky doubt that I was missing something.

Part of this was a mindset I have had from an early age. I was typically the outlandish kid who always had weird ideas of how to accomplish a task. I was made fun of both at school and home for my outlook and determination to do something differently. As a result, I developed insecurity with any product born out of what I thought was my crazy mind. I don't think like others, so how could I create success in a world that opposes the "different." What I needed (but didn't want) was something to put Sprint Recruiting to the test. It would need to be something entirely out of my control and force us to reevaluate the methodology's validity in the most extreme circumstances.

In March of 2020, my team and I prepared for a four-day summit to celebrate the wins achieved through the Sprint Recruiting company-wide rollout while also planning for the remaining part of the year. Of course, COVID19 threw all of our in-person plans out of the window, but that did not keep us from evaluating the wins and obstacles of Sprint Recruiting. COVID19 also brought us a unique opportunity to stress test this new methodology in one of the weirdest economic phases most of us had ever encountered.

What did we learn? Sprint Recruiting is even more important during the COVID crisis. We had some mindset setbacks both with our client and on our team, but it helped us reorganize around the four principles that drive the success of Sprint Recruiting. Here are the principles and what we learned during COVID.

The Sprint drives focus.
Perhaps one of the most significant mindset shifts experienced by both new recruiters and clients is the understanding of reviewing positions in a sprint time frame. Our sprints are two weeks beginning on a Wednesday. Most of our clients were still early in the adoption process when COVID hit. While I thought this would be a setback for us, it proved to work in our favor.

Situations were changing so fast during the early months of COVID. Just as we decided on one course of action, state or local mandates changed our plan or required us to reallocate our focus to other parts of the company. The Sprint allowed us to move as quickly as the market and clients demanded. Before the pandemic, clients typically struggled with the narrow focus of the two-week sprint. Still, with all of the noise and confusion brought by COVID, Sprint Recruiting's simplicity helped clients focus on what should be accomplished during a manageable timeframe.

Points Drive the Priority

As COVID19 bore down on the nation and affected the number of openings company's had, we were able to work with the same methodology we had been using before the pandemic to maximize efforts.

In one of our business units, we partially opened our offices to the public to serve their needs because our business is essential. The point system helped provide further context and focus for our executives during our point allocation call. One of our executives informed his team the only positions to receive points were those deemed most critical to keep our offices open. What was most interesting to me was the internal pushback our clients gave each other during our calls. Rather than unrealistic expectations placed on my team, I listened as the executive on the call directed and sometimes redirected his or her team to define priority.

The role of Talent Acquisition was to provide a progress update for the last sprint and provide insight to the discussion. We were not responsible for determining or guessing which roles were most important. After 15 years in the industry playing the guessing game, it was a beautiful moment to see this process work in our favor.

WIPs Maintain Efficiency

The COVID Confusion (my term) brought even more noise to the recruiting process. When our company forced most to work from home, it caused many hiring managers' adjustments when it came to interviewing. The WIPs allowed us to keep our managers focused on keeping the process moving efficiently. We had pockets of candidates who were able to interview with multiple managers across business lines where before, we were unable to work this kind of magic. Part of this was because of the COVID economy, and the candidate market drove the other.

WIP limits kept our recruiters and managers working toward a common goal, despite the COVID confusion. We had a couple of instances where we were at our WIP limit early in the sprint and waiting for managers' feedback. It was when our team decided to update our status list to include WIP LIMIT. The status is visible to all and serves as a trigger for us to dig deeper into where the process is broken and work to fix it. We were able to train our hiring managers to work within the confines of WIPs, which leads to one area that proved to be a significant obstacle for us during the pandemic.

Feedback Keeps the Process Going
Feedback is the energy that keeps the engine going. It helps us determine if our search strategy is on point or needs refining. Feedback opens space in our funnel to pull more qualified and vetted candidates into managers' process to review. All of this starts and stops with timely manager feedback. The COVID confusion and noise seemed to present the largest obstacle in this principle. Understandably, managers were pulled in different directions while also learning to manage a virtual workforce. The multiple and changing deadlines created havoc for our managers.

The agreement in our Sprint Recruiting Process is for feedback within 48 hours of presenting or interviewing candidates. As you can imagine, COVID-19 complicated this process. Some managers were quarantined without notifying the recruiting teams, which created a strain on our candidate experience.
Our team regrouped with our clients two sprints into the crisis to address the feedback obstacle. In some units, we created interview panels that determined candidates' job fit

and made hiring decisions on behalf of the rest of the team. Other areas leveraged reports showing which managers were understaffed and unable to interview to allow recruiters to create alternative ways to get the feedback needed to continue the process.

The primary lesson learned from our obstacles was the commitment both the recruiting team and the clients had to the Sprint Recruiting methodology. We knew it worked pre-COVID, so when one of the pillars presented challenges, we worked in PARTNERSHIP with our client to keep the process moving. COVID-19 taught us how Sprint Recruiting was even more useful during a crisis. Sure, we had to make some slight adjustments, but the core methodology and success factors did not change.

It's exciting to report that our time to fill in most of our critical areas decreased due to less open jobs and more focus on those deemed most vital. As we reopened our retail units, we could realign resources to critical areas with the most risk to our client experience and deliver quality candidates in shorter periods. We tested new recruiting team models to determine if we could experience efficiencies while continuously focusing on how our clients defined success during our sprints.

The unplanned stress test also gave me the confidence to write this book and share our journey with you. It was a mindset shift I had to implement on myself that wasn't the most exciting part of the process. I'll have to warn you that leading the mindset change is one of the most exhausting yet rewarding aspects of Sprint Recruiting. Be ready for some significant obstacles, but I challenge you not to give up. Once you shift your team and client's mindset, your recruiting utopia isn't too far behind.

The Sprint Recruiting Mechanics

With the methodology in mind, let's begin plotting your journey to a successful implementation. The next few pages are the result of trial and error my team experienced. We will discuss the importance of reporting and designing your meeting cadence to create opportunities for iterative growth each sprint.

Measure what counts

For the metrics to be impactful, there are a few rules to remember. The metrics' goal is not to track who didn't do their job but to drive improvement in the team. Here are some guidelines to remember:
- *The team uses the metric* – Metrics should not be imposed or measured by management. The metrics should be used voluntarily by Agile teams to learn and improve.
- *The metric includes conversation* – Metrics should not just be numbers. They should be the starting point of a discussion about process and roadblocks affecting the team. It allows for excellent team buy-in and an opportunity for managers to provide continuous, impactful feedback.
- *The metric is used in tandem with other metrics* – Even a great metric might lead to tunnel vision if used in a vacuum. It is counterproductive because it will incentivize teams to maximize that metric at the expense of all else. Using several metrics together provides a balanced picture of progress and allows the team to have healthier discussions during the Retrospective meeting.
- *The metric is easy to calculate and understand* – Metrics that are overly complex or not fully understood, even if they provide useful insights about a team's work, are not valuable for guiding day-to-day activities. So you don't need a report with Vlookups, fancy charts, interdependent formulas. Please keep it simple but measurable.

So with that, let's get into some of the metrics used in sprint recruiting.

Open versus Hired Chart
Remember, the mindset shift from traditional to sprint recruiting takes a while. You will not be able to convince your clients or even your team to let go of the only metrics they've known. Tracking the open versus hired sprint to sprint will help with the adoption process while also showing the sprint recruiting value.

Leverage the open versus hired report as a contrast to the new values of Sprint Recruiting. We found once our clients began embracing the point system, the open versus hired report began to show more positive trends. We used this data to prove why the new methodology was more productive. As the business starts prioritizing positions, and your team uses this focus to create efficiencies, the byproduct is the ability to fill more jobs within two weeks. Without charting the progress, you will miss out on a critical tool to help transition out of the old and into the new way of thinking.

Sprint Burndown Chart
You'll need to show how many points were obtained during the sprint and how many remain. It helps the team celebrate the wins but identify what gaps remain. During the stand-up meetings, it is helpful to provide some clarity for what tasks need to be accomplished before the next meeting. This chart makes it instantly clear how much value has already been delivered and how close the team is to meet its commitment for that sprint.

Imagine a bar graph depicting how many points are assigned during each sprint. The bars may be level in most of your sprints but remember, clients have the option to expedite an important position each sprint by assigning an extra 100 points. If you have too many expedited roles, the chart's fluctuation will be easy to see and should initiate a conversation with your client regarding prioritizing points.

Now that you have your assigned points charted with the bar graph, you will now track your closed points, or points won with a line graph. This visualization quickly shows you the progress made in the sprint. It also helps you look at previous sprints to identify successful sprint patterns.

See the example below:

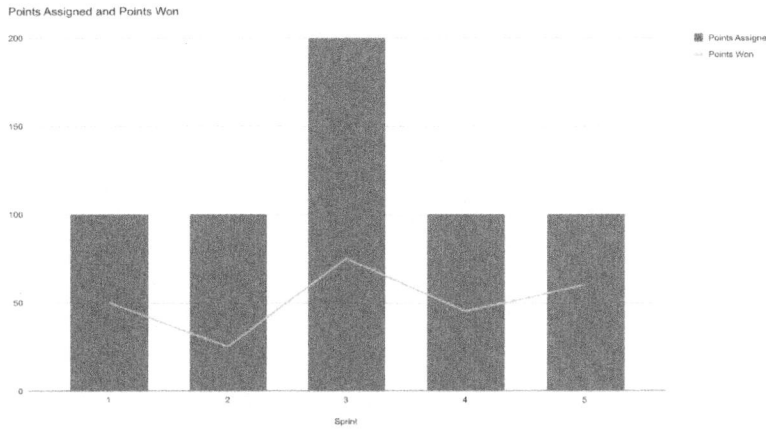

I use this chart daily to measure our progress and determine if we are on track to meet our client's definition of success. The simplicity of the chart allows sprint participants to understand some important metrics and assumptions quickly:

1. The average number of points obtained by the team is 50. This is the team's baseline and can identify a team's productivity throughout the sprint. At the one-week mark of every sprint, the team should have closed at least 25 points to be on target.
2. The third sprint had an expedited role since the number of points available is higher than the other sprints. Too many of these spikes would require the recruiting leader to challenge the client's thought process during the allocation process.
3. The second sprint was the lowest of the five charted. During the team's retroactive meeting, they would

need to determine what factors led to the dip in production. We have found there to be recurring obstacles presented by our processes or client schedules. It has allowed us to plan for these and amend our approach to the sprint.

The Sprint Burndown Chart is one of the most critical tools you will use throughout the sprint. Its simplicity allows sprint participants to improve performance with the passing of each sprint. As a leader, it will be the chart you use to determine gaps in the recruiting delivery process. Recruiters can quickly assess their ability to meet the needs of the client. Clients will use it to understand their part in the success of a successful sprint.

Extra Credit
Don't forget to track points for those roles closed during the sprint, not assigned points by the client. You'll need to follow all work done during the sprint, so work with your team to decide how many points will be given to non-sprint roles closed. Our team decided to use a cut-off point at a specific grade level of the job. Everything closed below grade X would be assigned 5 extra credit points, and everything above grade X would be 10. Our rationale was that some of the lower level jobs were easier and less time consuming to close, so they should only be 5 points. The more complicated roles should be double the point value since it was usually double the work.

Here's an example of how our chart looked after we began tracking the extra credit:

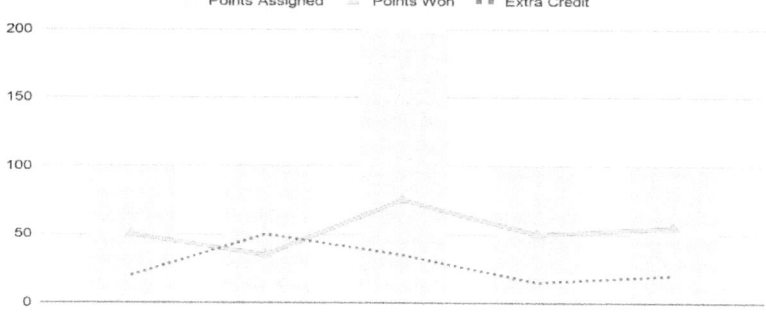

Notice in Sprint 2, the number of points obtained for critical roles (the green dotted line) is lower than the number of extra credit points (solid red line). This is an example of a sprint when non-sprint roles took precedence over those assigned points during the sprint. It's ok if this only happens during one or two sprints a quarter, but if the trend becomes the norm, you need to retrain your client to think about which roles are indeed a priority and assign points to them each sprint.

When we added this tracking metric, we were able to show data points to our client and discuss inefficiencies in the process. It also helped us avoid falling back into traditional recruiting traps when every job had a priority. Without this data, your team would appear unproductive and misaligned with the client's definition of success for the sprint. It's a valuable data point to ensure priorities are appropriately aligned, and everyone adheres to the sprint principles.

Sprint Velocity
Velocity measures how many points are attained by a team over the life of the sprints. It is a great tool to predict future productivity to prevent groups from committing to more than they can accomplish. It's essentially a result metric throughout sprints.

Using the sample chart above, we can see the team's performance over five sprints or ten weeks. The green trend

line notates the number of points won, displaying a rough average of 50%. As your trend lines begin to manifest in your reporting, you will be able to judge midway through a sprint at what percentage will keep you above your average.
If our velocity averages around 50% per sprint, on day 7, the team should be at or above 25%. This information guides the daily stand up to determine what obstacles will prevent the team from meeting the minimum. Discussing such information daily allows the team to realign themselves to help out in trouble areas. If one recruiter struggles to find quality candidates for a 50 point job, it will make sense to pull recruiters to help source and screen candidates.

Lead Time
This metric measures the total time from the moment a job enters the sprint until it's completed. Reducing lead time means greater efficiency. The Sprint Owner uses this particular metric to understand the length of time jobs spend in the process before providing value and predicting future commitments.

If you track information like the grade of a job or job family, you can add a filter to your report to focus on these critical elements. Tracking your lead time will allow you to set the proper expectations with hiring managers during the intake. Rather than promising to have the job filled in one sprint, your lead time for similar jobs may predict it takes roughly two sprints to fill the role. Discussing this with your hiring managers sets the proper expectation and decreases the amount of time spent meeting with managers who have unrealistic expectations. Let the data tell the story and help you manage these expectations.

Lead time also helps recruiting leaders better understand the capacity of the team. When a recruiter is assigned a critical role in a sprint, the leader should use the lead time to know if the lead recruiter will need someone to help either source for the essential role or take other roles to create capacity and focus. Without this metric, it is often too late for help to be given, and it negatively affects the client experience.

This metric can be tricky to track without proper reporting. I would encourage you to focus more on velocity during the first six months of your implementation. Treat lead time as the "cherry on top" metric you can dazzle your clients with once everyone is in the sprint recruiting mindset, and you've experienced the wins needed to gain buy-in from all involved.

Create your meeting schedules

I have never been a proponent of the "meeting for meeting sake" agenda. The meetings I suggest to you will hopefully eliminate duplicative sessions updating your client on the search. It is a streamlined, efficiency-first list of meetings for you to begin using to keep the process moving and free up some time.

The Daily Stand-Up
Let's first define what this meeting is not:
1. A review of your to-do list from yesterday and today.
2. A reading of your calendar
3. Long-winded pontification to prove you work hard
4. A time to fix major problems in systems, processes, etc.
5. "Just another meeting."

The stand-up meeting is a valuable tool if performed correctly. This should never turn into another meeting everyone dreads and only mildly participates. The actual value of the meeting is in its consistency, focus, and brevity.

For my team, we defined this time to answer the questions:
1. How did I move the needle yesterday on my critical roles/highest points?
2. How do I plan to move the needle today?
3. What is keeping me from accomplishing my goal?
4. Where do I need help from my team?

To quote one of my favorite presidents Franklin D. Roosevelt, the goal for this meeting is to "Be sincere; be brief; be seated." I would encourage anyone involved in the recruiting process to be involved in this meeting. We have found incredible value in our cross-functional team answering these three questions. This free-flow of communication allows every team member to hear each other's progress while also allowing them to work on any obstacles identified. It may be beneficial to have members of your support groups or HR business partners join so the entire team moves in the same direction. We tried this for a while, and it was effective until our teams got too large to accomplish brevity in our stand up.

Now you may be thinking, "A daily meeting? Who has time for that?". The key to the stand-up meetings is their efficiency. It's called a stand-up meeting because the early adopters realized that most people will keep their updates brief if they are forced to stand the entire meeting. Don't think of this as a daily bitch session when teams sit around a table blaming each other for obstacles or hang-ups. This meeting should not last any longer than 20 minutes, depending on the size of the team. A great way to keep these meetings efficient is to honor a simple rule: Everything you say should be valuable to everyone in the room. If a topic is highly complicated or time-consuming, call it out and have those involved schedule what we call an offline meeting to hammer out the details.

Everyone does stand-ups a little differently, but that's ok. There is not a one size fits all approach to being efficient with the stand-up meetings. You may find daily stand-up meetings overwhelming, but having one on Monday, Wednesday, and Friday is more productive. If so, go for it. The main objective is to create a schedule and environment for meaningful discussions to increase efficiency, enforce accountability, and identify obstacles.

One benefit I realized early on was my ability to know where we stood on critical roles at an organizational level. Before implementing Sprint Recruiting, I would often find myself blindsided by issues or client complaints. The daily stand-up meeting allows me to get ahead of potential problems and maintain a level of personal productivity throughout the week. Suppose I see a potential issue that needs attention. In that case, I will usually take the time to schedule something with those involved to discuss further and identify a solution before it gets escalated. This has saved me countless hours of reading email discourse and calming down angry clients.

The Recruiting Retrospective Meeting
After each sprint, the team meets to conduct a review of progress during the sprint. It should focus on what worked and what didn't during the previous sprint. It's a time of celebration and obstacle review. The goal of the meeting is to find ways to make the next sprint more productive. Imagine how impactful your efforts could be if you stopped at the end of a search to find scalable solutions to apply to future projects.

Unfortunately, in the traditional method, teams rarely celebrate what went well and exploring ways to scale those lessons for future projects. The retro meeting will retrain your team's mindset to look for the sprint wins and share them with the team. I've also noticed our team will usually work in independent groups on particularly interesting tips and tricks shared to discover ways we can scale them as a team. I rarely have to ask them to do it, which is the very definition of agility and why I enjoy our retro meetings.

The same is true for identifying the obstacles in the previous sprint. Avoid the tendency for this portion of the discussion to be a blame-game shit show. Identify the challenges and, as a team, work to identify ways to avoid or crush them in future sprints. It saves you and the team a lot of frustration and mental anguish. It's also a great way to identify what I call obstacle-trends. If I notice we have a trend of managers not giving feedback in the agreed-upon time frame, I take it to senior leadership to work with them to help minimize this obstacle. If there is a system or process that has created a delay in our ability to meet our goals, I work directly with the owners of those processes or procedures to find a solution.

The retro doesn't necessarily have to be another meeting on top of your stand-up meetings. Our team agreed that the last daily stand-up of the sprint is our retro. It helped us keep another meeting off our calendars. You may decide it's better to have a separate forum dedicated to the retro agenda, which is entirely up to you. Remember, this meeting cadence is about efficiency and agility. As long as your retro meets those two requirements, how and when you have, it is completely up to you.

Pro-Tip: Have a central document where you maintain a list of wins and obstacles. It will help you continue to scale what's working and avoid common obstacles. I've found creating a team Wiki for this is helpful to not only document but also allow the team to update as processes change.

Create a bi-weekly Retro/Allocation Call with the client

The beginning of the sprint is critical. You will need to establish a reoccurring, biweekly meeting with your clients to determine which positions are assigned priority. This meeting is also the meeting when you provide feedback on obstacles and successes from the previous sprint. Think of it as part retro and part allocation meeting. We typically spent roughly 15 minutes discussing the wins and struggles of the sprint for our calls before moving into the allocation portion of the meeting. Some of our clients require their direct reports to submit their allocation of points via email before the call, which allows us to ensure they're on the right track.

The added benefit we've noticed from this practice is that our executives usually push back on poorly assigned points with their directs, keeping us out of politics. Honestly, it's been kind of fun to watch our senior executives get a glimpse of the misguided directions we get from their direct reports. Again, this is where mutual accountability comes to play in sprint recruiting.

-Sidebar-

DO NOT let your clients disregard this meeting. If getting an update from you on recruiting activity is not important enough to take 30 minutes biweekly, then ice or hold their positions. I know it sounds harsh but trusts me it works.

We had one executive who would sometimes attend, sometimes be 15 minutes late, and sometimes not even give us the courtesy warning that he had a conflict with our STANDING MEETING BIWEEKLY.

So, being the petty but productive person I am, I told the team not to work on any of his positions that sprint. This executive's peers would get all of our attention since they made the time to meet with us and prioritize the work. Ironically, the executive was available for our standing call for the following sprint. I can't say he was pleased when we informed him we didn't work a lot in his region because we didn't know which roles were a priority. Of course, we didn't give him the cold shoulder, but there was more progress in the executive's peer regions.

He was offended, pissed, and slighted, but after he spent five minutes ranting about how his region's roles were important, I stopped him abruptly and agreed.

"Mr. Manager, I agree completely that you have important roles for us to fill. But I also have limited resources that I have to allocate over X number of regions for our company.

You've been late to our standing meetings, put us on hold for more important calls, and in the last sprint, you didn't even show up.

I'm sorry, but your words tell me your roles and prioritization are important but your actions are not supporting that. So now that we both agree you have important roles to fill, let's give some prioritization to this biweekly call so my team and I can give some prioritization to your roles. Agreed?"

There was an awkward silence on the call. I know two members of my team who were on the call were popping anti-acid pills from the confrontation but I remained calm. The executive, in his typical passive-aggressive way, said,

"Well, I guess we have an understanding, so now let's get to it before I get in trouble again."

It only took that one time for him to understand we were serious about aligning ourselves to the business's priority. If the business didn't deem recruiting as a priority, we would reallocate resources and time to those that would.

End of sidebar. Back to the point.

The agenda for the meeting is rather easy. It's the same agenda every two weeks:

- Review of the last Sprint.
- The client discusses what worked and what didn't.
- Recruiter discusses what worked and what didn't
- If needed, make plans to scale what worked and address what didn't.
- Discuss the upcoming sprint
- Review the open positions
- Allocate Points
- Agree to touchpoint meetings if needed
- Close the meeting

The first couple of sprint meetings will be rocky. Clients will want to use this time to talk about everything from Jonny who always comes in late to what's going on in the industry. Your job is to use the first two iterative meetings to ease them into sticking to the agenda.

The first line of business within our firm to go on sprint recruiting had an executive I enjoyed working with. I thought it would be a slam dunk implementing this biweekly meeting agenda. Forty-five minutes into the first meeting I realized I made a major blunder: I didn't send out the agenda for the meeting. We talked about the turnover in their group, the lack of qualified candidates in their market, the lack of budget they have to use, and of course, how recruiting sucked sometimes.

I barely got off the call with the points being assigned to roles which was the point of the damn call. I remember thinking to myself, "Well that was a cluster!"

The next call, I wised up. I sent the agenda on Thursday before our Monday meeting, along with a one-page graphic outlining the Sprint Process:

1. The business drives the priority-Points
2. The Sprint drives the focus-2 weeks
3. Feedback keeps the process moving
4. WIP keeps us in check

(Notice the precepts above have changed a little but remember, this was our first iteration.)

The next meeting went much smoother. When we began to drift off point, I gently reminded the partner we only had 30 minutes. We discussed what went wrong in the previous sprint but kept it brief. We talked about some wins we had by closing out two of the big five jobs identified in the previous sprint.

By the fourth iteration, we covered everything needed in roughly twenty minutes. The client loved the brevity of the meeting but appreciated the updates we provided on the key roles. We were able to allocate points in five minutes because the client had already spent some time with their direct reports discussing where the priority needed to be for the next two weeks. That was a "Hell Yeah" moment for me and the team.

Here are the critical components for your bi-weekly meeting to be a success:

1. **Everyone comes prepared**-It's critical for everyone on the call to be prepared for the call. As you get through your first couple, everyone usually finds their stride and the call runs more efficiently.

Hold everyone accountable for planning the discussion ahead of the call which is made easy by having the same three agenda items.
2. **Send your job report ahead of the call-** This was another lesson we learned after our second sprint. We leverage google sheets to track all of the open positions at the time the sprint begins. Most of our sprint calls are either Mondays or Tuesdays so we try to have our updates inputted and the report sent out to the POs by noon on Monday beginning a sprint. This helps the POs gather the information they need from their departments to help allocate the points during the call.
3. **Avoid chasing rabbits-** Part of the call is designed to discuss and overcome obstacles but do not let this derail your meeting. If a problem is too complicated to solve on the phone, everyone should agree to take it offline so the call progresses forward.
4. **Document the call and send it to the group-** This is a trick I use for every meeting I have but most especially for the sprint calls. A summary email to the group allows everyone to provide feedback and agree to the action items. This is where you capture any obstacles or successes that need more attention with a separate discovery or discussion meeting. It's also great to document the progress of your sprints and hold everyone accountable.

Keep it to 30 minutes-

This may seem like a monumental task but you'll be surprised how quickly the meetings will become as you progress through the Sprint Recruiting methodology. Remember, part of the process is to become more efficient, including your meeting cadence. Also, if you have weekly meetings with hiring managers or other distracting meeting schedules, try to consolidate them into this bi-weekly meeting. It'll save you time and energy but most important, focus, during the sprint.

Eliminate Duplicative Work

This cadence of meetings may sound a bit overwhelming, especially if you support multiple lines of business or executives. The challenge is not to squeeze these new meetings into your current litany of calendar events, but rather, to consolidate duplicative meetings. This will create some immediate efficiencies in your schedule and give more time to, I don't know...recruit?

In the beginning, many of the recruiters and I had weekly and biweekly meetings set with hiring managers who felt the need to meet to get updates. I had weeks consumed by these types of meeting requests which left little time to recruit and have something to update the managers. So when I began limiting the update meetings to either Mondays or Fridays, many of my executives were a little miffed, to say the least but time blocking saved my sanity.

You will have to design your meeting schedules in iterations to avoid client shock. In the first sprint, try to introduce a light version of your ultimate meeting cadence and work your way into it in every sprint. When we were piloting this with one of our high volume recruiting units, one manager expressed their concern with not having direct access to the recruiter at any given moment. The recruiter had anxiety that hiring managers would feel ignored and that it would impact their experience scores. During our first retrospective call with the client, both the hiring manager and recruiter admitted to how difficult the change was but both became quickly addicted to the results. The hiring manager began seeing 70% of her critical roles filled and quickly adjusted their behavior. Rather than emailing and texting throughout the day, the manager knew the recruiter's administrative blocks were from 8-9 am and 4-5 pm so she would engage the recruiter during those hours. It was an increase in productivity for both of them and a win for us.

The one on one meeting with your team

Traditional recruiting one on ones (101) were all over the place. Sometimes we went over updates, others we would talk about personal items, and other meetings accomplished anything. The sprint recruiting 101 has transformed these into a more defined agenda to include:

1. How close are you to meeting your sprint goal?
2. Where are we on your most critical roles?
3. What obstacles have you encountered this sprint?
4. How can I help you succeed?

The beauty of this agenda is that it doesn't change. I don't have to do a ton of preparation ahead of my 101s outside of reviewing the dashboard to be sure I know how far along the team member is in accomplishing the goal. I've also found I spend a lot more time listening during this style of 101 versus the traditional recruiting version.

Recruiters have also shared they like this format more because of its predictability and efficiency. We spend time keeping our client at the center of the discussion because we are focused on how the roles with points are progressing. Sure, we spend time talking about some obstacles caused by our clients but we spend more time on solution development than on griping about age-old complaints about hiring managers.

I also use this time to discuss developmental progress which team members enjoy. There have been times when some on the team could help with key projects or ideation sessions for the group. This developmental focus has allowed some team members to learn new skills applicable to both their job as a recruiting as well as outside of the recruiting world. This is just one of the many wins we've discovered in sprint recruiting.

Meeting Cadence Schedule

1. Daily Standup with your team
2. A Biweekly Retro meeting with your team
3. Biweekly Retro/Allocation call with your clients
4. Team one on ones
5. All other touchpoints should be on a Monday or Friday

Implementing this cadence will help you begin to realize the increase in productivity for you and your team. Sure, there'll be resistance from your clients but if you truly dedicate yourself to this cadence and time blocking, your client's concerns will wane as they begin to see more qualified candidates for their critical roles.

Your To-Do List

1. Set up your reporting.
    a. Remember to go to the Resource page on SprintRecruiting.com if you want to download a template
    b. Make the reporting work for you.
    c. Adopt a "One report to rule them all" approach and eliminate duplicative work.
    d. Be open to iterating your reporting until you find what works best for you and your clients.
2. Set up your meeting cadences
    a. Daily Standup with your team
    b. A Biweekly Retro meeting with your team
    c. Biweekly Retro/Allocation call with your clients
    d. Team one on ones
    e. All other touchpoints should be on a Monday or Friday
3. Innovate, iterate, and accelerate every sprint!

Final Thoughts-Answering WHY?

Let me introduce you to David, who started his own company in 1985. He discovered a need in a growing sector, and rather than merely opening a similar store to competitors, he decided to take a risk and go big. When his competitors offered only a couple of hundred products per store, this young company decided to provide 8,000. The competitors in the market used antiquated technology and processes, so David's Company invested in modern, computerized check-out processes. It positioned itself as the store of the future and quickly grew beyond its rivals.

David's company investments paid off, and only two years later, three large investors decided to help take the firm to the next level. After some management changes and opening 800 new stores, David's Company became the leading retailer in the space and an icon in its industry. It had reached the epitome of success, growing to over 1,000 stores and 8.4 Billion in revenue in 1994. Customers used its services as a benchmark for the few competitors in the space while suppliers threw themselves to have their product line on this powerful retailer's shelves.

Something happened to the firm as it continued to grow. The innovative and entrepreneurial spirit died under the weight of corporate processes and hierarchy. David's company began to focus more on how to stay at the top rather than on how to stay ahead of the industry. The economy was in the early stages of becoming an internet-driven market, but David's Company seemed committed to continuing its tried and true product delivery. When many of its rivals began closing, it attributed this more to its superiority than consumer behavior changes.

While David's Company was raking in cash and enjoying the view from its lofty position, Mark began a company of his own. He had become inspired by David's Company but realized there were some gaps in its business strategy. Motivated by the chance to start something new, Mark and a small group of colleagues entered the competitive market. It had a new, radical idea of delivering products to clients rather than merely waiting for them to come to their storefronts. Their concept seemed "out there" to most at the time because, unlike David's Company, Mark's Company built its platform on the web. It allowed clients to drive what products they wanted and when.

Rather than meeting in large boardrooms with oversized executive teams, Mark's Company met in a local hotel conference room. The culture was fast and seemingly erratic to those on the outside. The firm's commitment to innovation sometimes wreaked havoc on its financials, but the team was fueled by determination and passion. Unfortunately, the burst of the ".Com" Bubble in 2001 left the firm without funding from venture capital firms and in the red. While the business model and product had great potential, the firm would have to close its doors unless it received an influx of cash soon.

It was around this time that Mark's Company approached David to purchase them for 50 Million. Mark's company would become the online retailer for David's, expanding its reach far beyond the storefronts it depended on at the time. The data Mark and his presented to its potential buyer outlined just how profitable the deal could be, assuming the changes in consumer behavior towards more online purchases continued.
Despite the data, David turned the deal down. After all, why would an industry giant like David's Company want to spend that kind of money on an unproven startup? The firm could hire a team of developers to create an online store and save millions of dollars' worth of investment to accomplish the same goal. David and his management team decided to enter the online market two years after the meeting with Mark, but the company failed miserably and eventually went bankrupt in 2010. His firm's 25-year reign as the retailer icon crashed down as Mark's Company enjoyed record profits.

Like traditional recruiting, David's company, or more commonly known as Blockbuster, reminds me of the recruiting industry. The antiquated processes, addiction to

135

the industry's norms, and inability to innovate or evolve will bring about our downfall. I speak with many organizations that tout their new tools or new processes but find it incredibly hard to innovate how it can maximize client value or increase recruiting efficiencies. Blockbuster suffered from its inability to move quickly and meet the changes in consumer behavior. New ideas tended to be shot down in favor of keeping the normal overtaking a risk.

Unlike Blockbuster, Netflix has continued to stay true to its core value of keeping the client first and anticipating their needs. It has transformed from a DVD delivery service to an online content provider to, most recently, a production studio. Books and case studies have discussed the innovative culture and ability to move quickly from idea to product. It is known for its communicative culture and commitment to challenging the norm. Netflix's identity as an innovator and creator in the industry has allowed it to remain as one of the leading companies to work for and invest in for the last ten years.

Sprint recruiting is a major departure from the norms in recruiting. It challenges the age-old metrics, and its commitment to speed and quality is the very definition of a paradigm shift. We can no longer recruit as we have over the last ten years. Please take a moment to think about it. Five years ago, I didn't have a digital watch that could track my heart rate, answer the phone, receive texts, or tell me how long to wash my hands. Ten years ago, there were still pockets of people who used video cameras versus their cell phones. The quality of video and pictures has transformed so much in the last three years it's mind-blowing. All of this innovation and change has affected the candidates we recruit, yet many of us still feel committed to the old ways of recruiting.

Sprint recruiting has allowed our team to transform and evolve with our clients, the market, and our candidates. We're not married to only one way of doing a process or meeting a need. We've learned to fall in love with the problem we are trying to solve and not the solution. Instead of working for months on a new policy or procedure, we work on a framework and test it for one or two sprints. We take the feedback and either continue to iterate the idea or kill it. Sprint recruiting will allow you the time and focus on trying new things and aligning your success more closely with your client.

So if you've reached this part of the book and are still wary about trying Sprint Recruiting, ask yourself if it's worth the risk. You still have your old recruiting methods, so if you test the methodology and determine it isn't right for your organization, what have you lost? Conversely, imagine what would happen if it did work. Could you use some additional efficiencies on your team and candidate delivery? Would you be delighted to have mutual accountability for once? Wouldn't it be a relief to know at any given moment how closely aligned you are to the business's talent needs?

If you answered yes to any of those, I'd encourage you to take the risk and go for it. There are a ton of resources on SprintRecruiting.com to help you along the journey. I hope to hear about your success and cannot wait to see how the recruiting industry will transform over the next five years, with sprint recruiting leading the way.

In their own words

The success of sprint recruiting is largely due to the amazing team I work with. I thought it prudent to allow them to share some of their candidate feedback about the methodology. I did not force them to provide an edited answer so what you are about to read is legit. It's only fitting I give them the last word.

Interview with Corey

Corey joined our team in May of 2020 at the height of the COVID19 crisis. He had been in recruiting for a large cellular company prior to joining our team and had been working in sprint recruiting for at least five months at the time he was interviewed.

"In the traditional recruiting model, I would receive a requisition, post it for seven days, and screen all candidates who applied. If I did not get the needed talent, I would repost the position another seven days, repeating the steps until a successful candidate applies.

My initial thoughts of sprinting recruiting were that this might complicate what I like to do, which is recruiting and building relationships with my candidates.

The breaking moment that sprint recruiting was a breakthrough was when I was able to fill positions that were important to the business and were going to make an impact. I realized that sprint recruiting allowed my hiring manager to tell me what positions are critical, and sprint recruiting allowed me to influence my hiring manager when it came to a timely process for candidates, providing a great candidate experience.

My advice to someone new to sprint recruiting would be to embrace the change. Sprint recruiting is better for the business, hiring manager, and you as the recruiter's reputation."

Interview with Maura

Maura participated in the pilot for our high volume recruiting team in late 2019. I remember her initial excitement and anxiety during our training but what is more memorable was the moment she had her breakthrough. I thought it would be valuable to have her share her thoughts.

Explain how you worked in Traditional Recruiting.

My days in the Traditional Recruiting model were spent going through every job from oldest to newest. I followed the typical Intake, Post and Pray. I always felt it was necessary to touch EVERY position as they were all deemed top priority. I would check every job, see who applied, assess qualifications, screen, submit, schedule an interview with the hiring manager. Rinse, Repeat-all while taking numerous, unending calls from Hiring Managers who wanted to know any progress I had made on their role.

What were your initial thoughts about sprint recruiting when you were going through the training?

I was EXCITED and nervous. The excitement was to be able to FOCUS on specific jobs and have the Hiring Manager be a partner in the process. I was also excited to have so much accountability-it was invigorating. My angst came from having to sprint in a selected period of time. Two weeks sounded long but was it???

What were some of the mindset challenges you experienced?

I am a process-driven person and my only mindset challenge was time blocking. How was I ever going to be able to not answer the constant demands and issues of my clients? I am a people person! I want to assist ASAP and not make them wait!

At what moment did you have a breakthrough and realize sprint recruiting helped you? How did it help you?

I will never forget it. I had a particularly demanding and "overly engaged" Hiring Manager who always reached out, sometimes daily, on several things. Once I understood Sprint Recruiting and found my groove during SPRINT, I received a text saying "Am I allowed to bother you for a second?" That moment when that Hiring Manager understood I was focusing solely on what they defined as priority was an electric feeling and quite liberating. It helped me to be comfortable with the fact that I can no longer JUMP every second and be all over the place to please my client. I was on a mission that my clients had assigned me.

What would be your advice to anyone implementing Sprint Recruiting for the first time?

My advice to first-time sprint users would be to sit back and enjoy the uncluttering of your day and be ready to have a clear concise process. BUT, you MUST give it an open-minded chance...an honest chance.

Others from the team

I crowdsourced feedback to the questions below from the team.

How does the point system help the recruiting process?
Julie Allen
- *Establishing a point system with your business partner creates an opportunity for everyone to understand the requirements of the role as well as the competencies necessary for an individual to perform the job at a high level.*
- *Points help you prioritize how and where you should focus your time as well as your energy.*
- *If used appropriately points will help a Recruiter predict trends and should provide solid insights on succession planning.*

Kristie Adair

- *Prioritize. Recruiters and Recruiting Leaders have a visual goal for each LOB for each sprint.*

What are the biggest mindset shifts needed to make Sprint Recruiting successful?

Julie Allen

1. As a recruiter
    a. It is okay to not work on every Requisition at once-Work Smarter!
    b. You cannot be good at everything.
    c. You have to ask yourself what is most important. Several times per day.
    d. Dealing with Ambiguity is critical. And remember, you can only control what you can control. Be prepared and know things can and will need to change sometimes very abruptly.
2. For the hiring managers
    - Be flexible.
    - Invest. Hiring is one of the most important things you can do for yourself and your team. Don't cut yourself short.
    - Keep your word. If you agree to a meeting, an interview, offering feedback, etc. don't break your promise. Broken agreements will only hurt you in the long run and it definitely will not fill your critical role in an appropriate or timely manner.
    - Offer fearless feedback. It's okay to offer feedback if things are going well as well as if things aren't going well during the process. However, the most important thing you must remember when providing feedback is to

provide it specifically to your Recruiter. Feedback is a gift. You must give it directly to the individual you want to recognize or help to improve. When approaching a fearless feedback conversation always be clear, concise, and considerate.

Kristie Adair
- *Committing to becoming a trusted partner with your hiring managers and adapting recruiting efforts to match their business needs. By fully understanding their line of business and upcoming projects, recruiters will be able to better pipeline and strategize with managers. This way, everyone is on the same page and has the same goal.*
- *Developing an overarching mindset to staffing their teams. In Sprint Recruiting, managers must evaluate priorities based on strategic and tactical needs/timeframes and assign points based accordingly.*

Kate Harbison
- *Commit to the process - it is different but it works, trust that the role will be filled in a timelier manner if the process is followed by both Recruiter and Manager.*

What was the biggest adjustment you had to make as a recruiter going to sprint recruiting?

Julie Allen
1. *Open Communication and transparency are critical to your success. Recruiting sometimes leads people to want to over-promise or overcommit to someone or something. You can't allow yourself to get trapped by dogmatisms if you want to be successful in Talent Selection.*
2. *I had to learn that it is okay to say No to someone or something. It isn't always right to say Yes to*

something if you can't actually deliver on your promise.

Kate Harbison
Dedicated time blocks. Being respectful to the commitment of the points regardless of another manager or division reaching out.

Kristie Adair
Letting go! It's ok to focus on client-defined priorities and not to try and fill everything all at once. The number of fills doesn't always equate to appropriately staffed teams.

Other feedback or advice you might have for teams converting to sprint recruiting:
Julie Allen
If you could only do one thing it should be to focus your attention on educating the business and your leaders that every single member of the organization is responsible for Talent Selection. People are the fuel to any organization, therefore, why would we not do everything in our power to enhance our position, our growth, our successes, and our future. It starts with all of us. We're in this together!

Kate Harbison
Be open-minded to the significant shift in process. This is way beyond how we have done it before - it takes patience and commitment to learning. When you reach the point of going back to the old way, give it another chance and push through - you will be grateful you gave it a chance.

Kristie Adair
Lean in! This is a significant shift from traditional recruiting methods, but it will change your manager relationships as you become more of a staffing team

together rather than a recruiter and a manager. Individuality in roles transforms into a more team effort to achieve the same goal.

Bibliography

Ambler, Scott (12 April 2002). Agile Modeling: Effective Practices for EXtreme Programming and the Unified Process. John Wiley & Sons. pp. 12, 164, 363. ISBN 978-0-471-20282-0.

The Complete Guide to Time Blocking. (n.d.). https://todoist.com/productivity-methods/time-blocking

Darrell K. Rigby, Darrell K. Rigby Jeff Sutherland Hirotaka Takeuchi, Bradley Staats and David M. Upton, & Steven Spear H. Kent Bowen. (2017, March 21). Embracing Agile. https://hbr.org/2016/05/embracing-Agile

Darrell K. Rigby, . (2020, April 03). Agile at Scale. https://hbr.org/2018/05/Agile-at-scale

Francino, Y. (2019, January 22). Your first Agile sprint: A survival guide. https://techbeacon.com/app-dev-testing/your-first-Agile-sprint-survival-guide

Halperin, K. (2015, July 23). The Agile Recruiting Manifesto. https://www.ere.net/the-Agile-recruiting-manifesto/

Johanna RothmanAugust 1, 2. (2018, February 19). Five W's of Agile Recruiting. https://insights.dice.com/employer-resource-center/five-ws-of-Agile-recruiting/

MacLellan, L. (2018, October 10). This simple tweak to a standard request will make you a more effective leader. https://qz.com/work/1418504/brene-browns-advice-for-becoming-a-more-effective-leader/

Perell, K. (2020, October 07). 5 Ways to Cultivate an Entrepreneurial Mindset. https://www.entrepreneur.com/article/357163

Segue Technologies. (2020, April 13). 8 Benefits of Agile Software Development. https://www.seguetech.com/8-benefits-of-Agile-software-development/

Why Rejecting Candidates is Actually Good for Your Employer Brand. (2019, March 27). https://www.zippia.com/employer/rejecting-candidates-after-interview-is-an-essential-part-of-the-recruitment-process/

Why Rejecting Candidates is Actually Good for Your Employer Brand. (2019, March 27). https://www.zippia.com/employer/rejecting-candidates-after-interview-is-an-essential-part-of-the-recruitment-process/

Yong, E. (2014, January 15). Birds That Fly in a V Formation Use An Amazing Trick. https://www.nationalgeographic.com/science/phenomena/2014/01/15/birds-that-fly-in-a-v-formation-use-an-amazing-trick/

Printed in Great Britain
by Amazon